Entrepreneur® MENTOR SERIES

KILLER CUSTOMER CARE

How to Provide Five Star Service That Will Double and Triple Your Profits

GEORGE COLOMBO

EP
Entrepreneur®
Press

Editorial Director: Jere Calmes
Cover Design: Beth Hanson-Winter
Composition: CWL Publishing Enterprises, Inc., Madison, WI,
www.cwlpub.com

ISBN 1-891984-86-1

Library of Congress Cataloging-in-Publication Data

Colombo, George W.
    Killer customer care : five star service that will double and
triple profits (mentor) / by George W. Colombo.
        p. cm.
    ISBN 1-891984-86-1
    1. Customer services. I. Title.
HF5415.5.C624 2003
658.8'12--dc22

                                                    2003049406

Printed in Canada
09 08 07 06 05 04   10 9 8 7 6 5 4 3 2

CONTENTS

SECTION IV

Keeping Your Killer Customer Care Program on Track

A COMPELLING CASE

George Colombo and I strongly disagree on one fundamental point. Let's deal with that first. George believes that for a variety of reasons, customers are in control of business relationships and that this reality, which will only become more pronounced over time, must shape the priorities of every business leader.

I'm of the opinion that a whole lot of businesses have been treating you, me—and yes, George, you too—like dirt. Whether it's eBay's decision to provide no way for disgruntled customers to contact it, Intuit's decision to assume its customers are thieves, or the policy of every credit card company in existence—to offer prospects excellent interest rates only until they become customers, after which the rates get jacked through the roof—whichever of these depressingly common experiences you had last week, you're sure to agree with me, not George.

That's where George and I disagree. Where we agree is that you ought to treat your customers like royalty. The prevalence of shabby customer treatment makes the case for killer customer care even more compelling.

Here's why. If everyone were doing it, your best hope might be to survive among the wolves, eking out a living by chewing on squirrel scraps as you travel in the pack. As it is, by treating your customers well you'll be in elite company—if you have any company at all.

That's all you gotta do.

Oh, if it were only that easy!

When you start a company, there's just you and the customer. If you get much business, you hire a few employees, and you all deal directly with each other and with your customers, mind-melding about how to deal with situations as they arise. Then comes success, and with it the only two factors needed for failure: managers and policies.

To understand why managers are an essential ingredient for failure, you need do nothing more than play the children's game of telephone. No matter how well you think you've explained how you want employees to treat customers, it will be filtered through each manager's own thought process, bonus incentives, biases, and ego. What comes out the other side might match what you'd hoped for, but the more layers of management you have, the less likely that is.

Then there's the policy manual – an attempt to translate personal thoughts, opinion, hopes, dreams, and wisdom into the corporate version of a legal code. Once a policy exists, taking care of customers takes a back seat to adhering to the policy manual. "I can't do that for you, sir. It's against our policy," is the death knell of customer loyalty. Your customer hears it and knows that your employee must choose between taking care of his problem and keeping her job. Because her manager—remember those managers you have?—will fire her for violating policy.

What chance do you—as a business owner—have?

That's what George's book is for: To give you a chance. Anyone can write a book describing how your business should behave to maximize customer retention and wallet-share. That's easy to prove. Just take a look at the business book section at your local bookstore. You'll find lots of 'em. If you read one, chances are good you'll come away inspired by the potential for additional profits that come from improving and extending customer relationships.

Chances are equally good you'll wake up the next morning wondering what, exactly, you should do to make it all happen.

There's a fair distance between a wonderful concept and disciplined execution.

And that's the difference between what you have read and what you're about to read. The only problem you'll have reading *Killer Customer Care* is finishing it, because I don't see how you can finish even one chapter without wanting to put down the book and implement the thoroughly practical suggestions you just encountered.

So here's a piece of advice. While there are times that resisting temptation is a good thing to do, this isn't one of them. Don't resist—go ahead, put down the book, and take action. Your customers won't complain. I promise.

Your employees won't complain, either. They want to provide killer customer care. You have to create an environment in which they can and in which they are rewarded for doing so instead of penalized by their managers for violating the policy manual.

So go ahead and implement the ideas you like as you encounter them. This is a practical book, designed to let you do so.

But you should read the whole book, because while the ideas in it can work on their own, they have much more power when carried out as part of a thorough, integrated program.

And in fact, you must, because while each idea is useful, many will have no staying power unless reinforced with others. For example, giving employees spot cash rewards for exceptional customer treatment works wonders but can fizzle into a corporate entitlement if not quickly backed with the deeper structural change of a revised compensation system.

Or, to take a different example, you'll gain advantage through a focused effort to set customer expectations—what "branding" is supposed to be about but rarely is. Compared to the benefit you'll experience by also implementing programs that ensure everyone in your company understands and knows how to deliver on those expectations, though, the initial advantage is minor.

Somewhere, the word "synergy" is begging to be included in the discussion, but let's not let it in. "Synergy" is for high-concept consultants, after all.

The book in your hands is for practical businesspeople who are ready to take action instead of just thinking great thoughts. Presumably, you're one of them.

—Robert Lewis
President, *IT Catalysts*

WHY KILLER CUSTOMER CARE?

You might be thumbing though this introduction in the aisle of your favorite bookstore, or you might be reading it online. Chances are, you're wondering if this book would be worth your time or if it contains the kind of practical information you'd be able to use to grow your business and increase your profits. After all, there are more business books out there than you'll ever have time to read, and they are all competing for your time and attention. Let's face it; the concept of customer care is not exactly news. Why, then, is this particular book worth your time?

Killer customer care is the ultimate competitive differentiation for businesses in the twenty-first century. It encompasses tactics that are immediately accessible to businesses of all sizes and in all kinds of different industries. These tactics are simple, straightforward, and can immediately impact the way your customers experience your business. At the same time, there is a strategic element to killer customer care that is challenging but worth the effort required to master it. It will enable you to significantly differentiate your business and leave your competitors hopelessly in the dust. In this book, you're going to learn about both aspects of this extremely important topic.

Let me share with you three undeniable truths that provide the foundation for everything else you'll read in this book. Take a moment to consider them. Then, you'll be in a better position to decide whether or not this book is for you.

Undeniable Truth #1: Customer Care Is More Important Than You Realize

Most business owners and managers are certainly willing to pay lip service to the importance of customer care. They instinctively recognize that it is a significant aspect of building their businesses. What they don't realize is that customer care can be their single most important weapon for competing in a crowded and highly competitive marketplace. It's no exaggeration to say that customer care is rapidly becoming the battleground on which the very fate of your business will be determined.

The new reality of today's business environment is that you can no longer count solely on the quality of your company's products and services to bring about success in the marketplace. In all types of different industries, the quality of your product or service is no longer enough to create a

Good, Fair, and Poor

A few years ago, one of the leading consumer magazines was preparing to publish one of its customary product evaluations. The format called for a review of every major manufacturer's CD players, ranking each product as "Good," "Fair," or "Poor."

When the results came in, however, the editor was astonished to find that there were no "Poor" choices left in the entire product category and that the most significant differences between "Fair" and "Good" categories were product features that were a function of price. In other words, the qualitative differences between competitors in an entire product category had virtually disappeared!

significant competitive advantage. Does that mean that quality isn't important? Of course not! In many ways, quality is probably more important that ever. It's just that quality now is simply the ante required to stay in the game.

The same is true of many of the other ways in which companies have traditionally competed. Differentiation on the basis of technology, for example, is almost impossible to sustain. It's even truer of attempts to differentiate yourself on the basis of price, which is almost always a fatally flawed strategy. If you're looking for a way to differentiate yourself strategically, you're going to have to look somewhere else. For many businesses, customer care will prove to be the only viable answer.

Undeniable Truth #2: It's Highly Likely You're Not as Good at Customer Care as You Think

Over the years, I've worked with the owners and managers of hundreds of businesses in a variety of different industries. A few of those businesses were outstanding at customer care, most were fair, and a handful of them were downright dreadful. Whatever the objective reality was, however, when I sat down and spoke with the owners and managers of these businesses, each one insisted that, whatever other shortcomings his or her business might have, the company provided terrific customer care. The degree to which these otherwise rational businesspeople were willing to kid themselves about their customer care performance was nothing short of amazing and, to tell you the truth, more than a little amusing!

So, how well does *your* business do when it comes to customer care? The truth is that it might not do as well as you think. In fact, it's not easy to know. For one thing, the overwhelming majority of customers who aren't satisfied

> *I have realized that there are certain qualities about which people simply cannot evaluate themselves objectively. (If you don't believe me, try asking any young men you might know if they're good drivers.) In certain areas—customer care included—no one will admit to being below average, and virtually no one will admit to being merely average. Instead, almost everyone will tell you that they're far above average, a situation your friendly neighborhood statistician will tell you is impossible!*

with how they're treated will not take the time to track someone down in order to register a complaint. They will simply disappear one day and never return. You'll never be quite sure what happened or why.

Even if a dissatisfied customer mentions a complaint to one of your employees (a more likely scenario than their complaining directly to you), chances are you'll never hear about it. For a variety of reasons, your employees are more likely to try to shield you from bad news than to share it with you, especially if they're involved in what caused the complaint in the first place.

A final barrier between you and the truth about your business is the fact that, for most businesses, customer care performance varies over time and usually depends on the particular employee with whom your customer happens to interact. Most of the time, it's OK. Occasionally, it's great. And, every once in a while, it's abysmal. Even if you're resolute about finding out how well your business is performing, you'll still be faced with a challenge that's similar to trying to guess what an entire jigsaw puzzle looks like when you have only a few pieces and you're not exactly sure even how those pieces fit together.

Undeniable Truth #3: Many High-Impact Customer Care Strategies Can Be Implemented Quickly Without a Huge Investment

Some business owners and managers are reluctant to get started with customer care because they think it will be complicated or cost too much. It's certainly true that some elements of a comprehensive customer care initiative will require careful planning and a significant investment. (That investment will deliver a handsome return, by the way, so don't let yourself be put off.) On the other hand, there are lots of high-impact strategies and techniques that you can implement tomorrow if you want to. You find them throughout this book. The only thing that's required is your decision to use customer care as a competitive weapon in your market and the determination to get started.

There's one last point I want to make before we get going. You may be wondering why the title of this book is *Killer Customer Care*. Isn't that title a little—aggressive? Well, yes! Beyond the obvious definitions of "killer," there are a couple of secondary definitions that I had in mind when I chose the title:

> *n.* Something that is extremely difficult to deal with or withstand: an exam that was a real killer.

> *adj.* Having impressive or effective power or impact; formidable: had a killer smile; made killer profits.

If you think of customer care merely as an incremental improvement on the ambience your customer experiences at your store or in your business, then you should know that you and I are definitely not on the same page! On the other hand, if you're looking for a business strategy and a set of tools that will create a clear advantage in the market-place—something that makes a big and immediate difference in your business results—and if you want to present your competitors with the kinds of challenges that are almost impossible to overcome, then this book is for you.

In Section I, you'll explore ways in which a killer customer care strategy can impact your business's performance and profitability. In Section II, you'll discover how to prepare your business for a dramatic customer transformation. In Section III, you'll learn the specific tactics and techniques you'll use to implement a killer customer care plan in your business. Finally, in Section IV, you'll learn how to keep your customer care program permanently on track.

That's the agenda. So, if you're ready to see how to make this ultimate business strategy part of your business, let's get started!

Dedication

To Sandy.

I can't improve on how Gladys Knight put it: You're the best thing that ever happened to me.

Acknowledgments:

I am grateful for the indispensable contributions that several people made to the process of conceiving and creating this book

Jere Calmes' patience as he shepherded this project along was seemingly inexhaustible. Ciree Lindstrom provided a keen eye and a deft touch to a manuscript that benefited tremendously from her attention.

Ginger Conlon and Ginger Kernachan both gave me valuable input and important advice as this book took shape. My writing has improved tremendously over the years as a result of the guidance I've received from both of them.

I was fortunate enough to be able to develop and hone these ideas over a long period of time with several people who are close personal friends as well as valued business colleagues. Bob Lewis, Steve Osborne, Barry Trailer, and David Wenning have all shaped my thinkinf and kept me intellectually honest.

As a friend and consigliere, Jim Jeter is in a class by himself.

And, finally, every day Anthony and Joseph put everything else in its proper perspective. They are my heros.

SECTION I

▲ ▲ ▲

THE ONE CRITICAL FACTOR FOR BUSINESS SUCCESS IN THE 21ST CENTURY

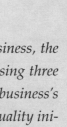

THE UNIQUE AND OVER-RIDING IMPORTANCE OF KILLER CUSTOMER CARE

CUSTOMER CARE: IT'S WHAT PAYS THE BILLS

As a senior manager who is concerned with building your business, the most important decisions you make every day are your choices about using three crucial—but finite—commodities: your time, your attention, and your business's resources. You could focus on product development; you might choose quality initiatives; or you could even choose to focus your efforts in the ever-popular area of sales and marketing. Over time, all of those areas—and more—will demand your attention.

But I want to persuade you that, in today's hypercompetitive business environment, there's one area that deserves the lion's share of your time and your attention. Your focus on that area will generate a healthy, tangible return on your investment and it will enhance the effectiveness of everything else you do. That focus, of course, is on customer care. To be even more specific, it's on a combination of strategies and techniques that will elevate your efforts to the level that I refer to as killer customer care.

What you're about to learn goes far beyond teaching your employees to smile and say, "Have a nice day." Killer customer care refers to a combination of principles, ideas, and techniques that are designed to consistently and systematically enhance the depth and breadth of your business's relationship with its customers. It is part tactics, part strategy. On a tactical level, it is so simple that you can get started immediately. On a strategic level, it is powerful enough to create virtually impregnable barriers between your customers and your competitors.

The Case for Killer Customer Care

So what makes killer customer care so important? The

Care vs. Service

You might be wondering why we are talking about "customer care" instead of using the more familiar term, "customer service." Is the use of "customer care" just a semantic device? Or is there a real, significant difference between customer care and customer service—one that is significant? Actually, the difference is far deeper than mere semantics. The two terms have dramatically different connotations in describing the nature of your business's relationship with its customers.

"Service" suggests something that is transactional, functional, and finite. When you complete a service for a customer, the completion of that service brings you back to square one, regardless of how competently you might have performed. If you're lucky, you might have an incremental advantage when your customer looks for that service again, but you haven't created a decisive advantage for yourself relative to your competitors. "Care," on the other hand, suggests a deeper, ongoing relationship. If you care for your customer, then you're preempting the competition. Service is what you do to your car; care is what you do for someone in your family. Although customer service might have been adequate in the past, customer care is decidedly more appropriate for describing effective customer relationships today. As you integrate the principles, ideas, and techniques from this book into your business, the term care will express your vision more clearly to your employees and help keep your efforts on track.

short answer is it will make your business more profitable. And if it's done correctly, with discipline, over a long period of time, it can make your business dramatically more profitable. This is not something that's "touchy-feely" or "soft." Undertaken resolutely, killer customer care will provide you with a generous return on your investment of time, effort, and money, one that will withstand rigorous scrutiny from even the most skeptical observer.

The tangible return on your investment in killer customer care will come in four basic areas:

- Killer customer care improves your business's overall margins by fostering the kind of increased repeat business that lowers your overall cost of sales.
- Killer customer care highly leverages the performance of your company's marketing programs by consistently creating word-of-mouth referrals.
- Killer customer care enhances your company's product development efforts by connecting you more closely to what your customers need and want.
- Killer customer care protects your company's investment in sales and marketing by ensuring that new customers have a reliably positive experience with your business.

Killer Customer Care Improves Your Overall Margins

When most managers think about growing their business, they naturally gravitate toward a strategy of improving sales by adding new customers. There's no question about the fact that expanding a business's customer base is important, but it is often done at the expense of the business's performance on the even more important bottom line. There are several reasons for that unfortunate fact but the most significant reason is that there are usually hefty costs involved in acquiring a new customer. In fact, for many businesses, customer acquisition is a losing proposition, at least on the front end. It is increasingly common for a business to spend more money acquiring a new customer than it makes on its initial sale to that customer.

Years ago, such an approach would have been considered too risky. In today's hypercompetitive environment, though, it's simply not optional. New customers are difficult (and expensive) to acquire. The investment required to find each new customer can be justified only by looking at the total lifetime value of that customer. A sound underlying strategy depends on making the relationship profitable by enticing the customer to come back for additional purchases, thereby amortizing the high cost of customer acquisition over time.

Ah, there's the rub! You might have the resources to make the investment necessary to attract a new customer and the patience to wait before you start to realize a return on that investment. What you don't have—what you can *never* have, of course—is a reprieve from your competitor's relentless efforts to lure that hard-won customer away. If you're not able to hold on to your existing customers consistently, your business's profitability will suffer from the cost of constantly needing to find new customers to replace the ones that got lured away. In other words, if you can regularly and reliably turn first-time customers into repeat customers, you will enhance your margins and significantly increase your profitability.

Killer customer care is the most powerful strategy around for retaining your existing customers while simultaneously increasing the average size and frequency of their purchases. It is effective not only at enhancing your top-line revenue (more about that later) but also in its unique ability to do so while simultaneously enhancing your margins.

Killer Customer Care Highly Leverages Your Marketing Programs

In the world of marketing, a spontaneous word-of-mouth referral is the ultimate achievement. Of course, not all referrals are spontaneous. Most referrals are the product of some kind of incentive offered by the marketer for the referral. The basic formula for incentive-generated referrals is a familiar one—"Bring a friend and get …"—and it can be reasonably effective when implemented properly.

But the difference between an incentive-generated referral and a spontaneous one is considerable. Mark Twain once said, "The difference between the right word and the almost-right word is the difference between the lightning and the lightning-bug." The difference between an incentive-generated referral and a spontaneous one is kind of like that. They might seem similar at first glance, but one is merely pleasant while the other is irresistibly powerful.

Of course, in the normal course of events a spontaneous referral is a relatively rare thing. Think for a moment about your own history and consider a couple of questions. Over your lifetime, you've been the customer of hundreds of different businesses in dozens of different industries. How many times have *you* been motivated to give a spontaneous referral? If you're like most people, chances are it hasn't happened too often.

What, then, accounted for the difference between the overwhelming majority of businesses you've patronized and those select few that motivated you to give a spontaneous referral? There were probably two factors that tipped

A spontaneous referral happens when one of your customers, with no specific incentive to do so, grabs a friend or colleague by the lapels and, with passion and conviction, says something like, "Listen, you've really got to try this place."

When that friend or colleague visits your business (and, chances are excellent that they will, indeed, make the time to visit after such a referral), he or she will arrive with high expectations and low sales resistance. All of the marketing mechanisms built into your business will be even more effective than usual because your referral customer will be even more receptive than usual.

the scales in favor of a business that inspired you to refer a friend or colleague. The first is that you personally had a terrific experience there, one that went beyond what you expected and what you typically experienced at other, similar businesses. The other factor, one you probably didn't recognize consciously when you made the referral, was that you had reason to believe your experience was not unique. At some level, you believed that if your friend visited that business, his experience would be as positive as yours. Spontaneous referrals only happen when both of those factors are present.

The strategies and tactics that make up killer customer care address both of those factors. When you implement the ideas in this book, your customers will enjoy remarkably positive experiences with your business. And they'll be confident in referring friends and colleagues because they'll know that their positive experiences at your business were the rule, not the exception.

Killer Customer Care Enhances Your Company's Product Development Efforts

There's an old adage that offers this caution: Before you climb a ladder, make sure it's leaning up against the right wall. The truth underlying that warning is illustrated by the long list of companies that have spent large amounts of time and money developing products and services their customers neither needed nor wanted. Certainly, an occasional misstep is unavoidable, even under the best of circumstances, and it's also true that those companies that characteristically live on the cutting edge of technology must often proceed into uncharted territories. Still, it's remarkable how many costly and sometimes embarrassing mistakes could have been avoided if companies had simply

A Role Model: Dell

In an industry where most of the players have at one time or another looked like financial piñatas, Dell Computer Corporation has been incredibly sure-footed in its product development and operations over a long period of time. Some competitors and industry analysts have attributed the company's success solely to its direct sales model. However, repeated attempts to emulate that success have yielded disappointing results.

What's escaped everyone's attention, in spite of Michael Dell's consistent straightfor-wardness on the point, is that *Dell simply listens to its customers more closely than anyone else in the business*. Michael Dell has repeatedly pointed out that the direct sales model doesn't confer any special advantage by itself. What makes it powerful is Dell's determination to take advantage of the fact that it's communicating directly with its customers every day.

Dell listens to what its customers want and deliberately distills that insight into a desirable product catalog that drives consistent profitability.

done a better job of listening—and I mean *really* listening—to their customers.

A fundamental tenet of killer customer care is that customers set the standards for success on their terms—not yours. A minor, but instructive, example of this—one that's familiar to most business travelers—is the hotel chain that deludes itself into thinking that a chocolate mint on the pillow at night or a bowl of cookies at the check-in desk represents a meaningful effort at customer care. In fact, the mint and the cookies are trite, and they're usually discarded. When real customer care issues go unresolved, those symbols of faux attentiveness can be downright annoying.

As your company learns to genuinely and consistently listen to its customers (utilizing techniques described in later chapters), you will avoid these missteps. And if you learn to listen purposefully and skillfully, you'll be able to emulate Michael Dell's example and regularly turn your insights into a set of products and services that decisively set you apart from your competitors.

Killer Customer Care Protects Your Company's Investment in Sales and Marketing

As we saw earlier, it's easy to gravitate toward a focus on sales and marketing when you're looking to build and/or grow your business. But if you undertake a massive sales and marketing effort before your customer care plan is in place, you might actually be doing more harm than good to the long-term health of your business. This may seem counter-intuitive, but more sales could actually be the *last* thing you need!

It is axiomatic that dissatisfied customers are far more vocal about your business with their friends and colleagues than satisfied customers. The results of several studies

Poor Customer Care and the Power of the Internet

Consider the story of Tom Farmer and Shane Atchison, two weary technology consultants from Seattle who tried to check into a Houston hotel in the wee hours of the morning not too long ago. Despite the fact that Farmer and Atchison had "guaranteed" reservations, the hotel had no rooms available. Far worse than the administrative lapse, however, was the fact that the night clerk, a hapless employee named Mike, was indifferent to their plight and distinctly unapologetic.

Until very recently, Farmer and Atchison would have vented by telling their story to a few friends and colleagues. In today's wired world, though, technology has exponentially increased the power of dissatisfied customers. Farmer and Atchison used Microsoft PowerPoint to create a devastating 17-screen "graphic complaint," titled "Yours Is a Very Bad Hotel," which they sent via e-mail to the hotel and copied to three of their friends.

The "viral" nature of communications on the Internet allowed their complaint to be disseminated quickly to thousands of business travelers all over the country. In short order, Farmer and Atchison received more than 4,000 e-mail responses, national press coverage, and attention from the entire hospitality industry in the wake of their missive. (You can likely find a copy of the presentation by typing "Yours is a very bad hotel" into the Google search engine.)

indicate that satisfied customers might tell one or two of their friends about their experience with your business (although killer customer care can improve that number substantially), but dissatisfied customers will complain to as many as ten people. That last number is conservative. It doesn't reflect the recent and dramatic empowerment of customers through the enhanced communications capabilities of the Internet.

So, if some significant percentage of customers who show up at your business are treated with hostility or indifference, would more customers help or hurt your long-term prospects? A pretty good case can be made that more customers would actually hurt because they ultimately are transformed into a larger contingent of vocal detractors.

A solid foundation of killer customer care skills will prevent your sales and marketing efforts from becoming counterproductive. You'll be confident that the resources you put into sales and marketing are being genuinely invested. You won't feel as though you're pumping water into a container that's leaking far faster than you can pump!

> *The story of two people's hotel problem became newsworthy because of Farmer and Atchison's clever PowerPoint presentation and the pervasive reach of the Internet, but it is certainly not unique. Employees like Mike, the uncaring night clerk, alienate customers every day.*

Welcome to the Twenty-First Century

In every market, in every industry, the unavoidable truth is that business is more competitive than ever before. Market forces have combined with technology to dramatically and irrevocably alter the balance of power between buyers and sellers. When customers had fewer options, businesses were able to dictate the terms of the marketplace. Today, customers hold all the cards, and they're upping the ante every day. Both business customers and consumers understand this implicitly and explicitly.

At the same time, the blinding speed at which markets adapt to competitive initiatives means it is becoming increasingly difficult to sustain a differentiation of your business based on traditional factors such as product innovation or price. The time it takes a competitor to knock off your new product or service has decreased dramatically. The window of opportunity in your marketplace for a new product or service might once have been six months. Now, it might be as little as six weeks—or even less. And, of course, there is no price point so low that you won't have a competitor ready and willing to match it. It should be increasingly clear to you that the only sustainable basis for long-term differentiation of your business is the degree to which you can make your customers feel positively connected to your business. As a result, your long-term success is highly dependent on the degree to which you're willing to embrace the principles of killer customer care.

There's one important bit of good news that will make a customer care strategy even more appealing. For a variety of reasons, customer care is a battlefield on which most of your competitors will not choose to compete. Like most businesses, they'll give lip service to customer care, and they may even genuinely believe they're already doing it well. But, like most businesses, they'll be wrong. If you choose to undertake this challenge, you may very well have an uncontested path to success—even dominance—in the one aspect of business that really counts in the long run: the ability to provide killer customer care.

Looking Ahead

Now that you've seen how important killer customer care is, let's take a look at what you can do to create a foundation for your success in this critical area. In Section II, you're going to learn about "Laying the Groundwork for Killer Customer Care."

SECTION II

▲ ▲ ▲

LAYING THE GROUNDWORK FOR KILLER CUSTOMER CARE

SETTING THE STAGE FOR YOUR KILLER CUSTOMER CARE PROGRAM

CREATING A CUSTOMER CARE CULTURE ◀

There are some tasks that just can't be done in small steps. If you're undertaking one of these tasks and try to do it in half measures, you'll inevitably wind up doing yourself more harm than good. Consider a guy who is standing on a precipice with a six-foot long chasm in front of him. He's never going to get to the other side by taking a couple of three-foot jumps. Either he's going to get there with one big leap or he's not going to get there at all.

That's an instructive metaphor to keep in mind as you prepare to instill the principles of killer customer care into your organization. A tentative, incremental commitment to transforming your business will simply not work. Either you're going to make killer customer care the touchstone for your company's approach to doing business in the future, or you will never succeed in creating meaningful change. Don't be misled by the fact that many of the strategies and tactics you're going to read about throughout this book are incremental—small, low-risk/high-impact steps you can take to move your company along the road to killer customer care. The first and most important step is an all or nothing proposition. When it comes to transforming your corporate culture, there is no such thing as an effective half measure.

Obviously, the prospect of undertaking a significant reconstruction of your corporate culture can be daunting, but companies that have already done it successfully have defined some specific steps that have been proven to work. This chapter will examine some important keys to making the leap successfully.

Understand and Acknowledge the Limitations of Your Employees' Perspectives

One of the reasons that killer customer care can be so tricky to achieve is that almost everyone in your organization has a vested, parochial interest in *not* taking care of your customer. This doesn't mean that they're bad people

Customer Care Challenges

Each department in your company has its own set of concerns that are seemingly at odds with a commitment to any sort of customer care:

- After a sale is made, the sales department is focused on making the next sale, not supporting the last one.
- The operations department resists anything that might interfere with the "big vanilla flow" of orderly operations.
- The accounting department wants tidy transactions that conform to straightforward rules.
- The service department wants to maintain an acceptable number of service calls per technician per day.
- The HR department wants the rules summarized neatly into a "Policies and Procedures" manual so all performance appraisals can be based on objective, defensible measures.
- Most executives and managers want to focus solely on their immediate sphere of influence, so that their success can be measured primarily on factors they can completely control.

Can you see the challenge here? Each department is trying to do the right thing based on its own perspective, its own concerns, and its own internal imperatives. The aggregate result can be a kind of perverse synergy-in-reverse. The whole (i.e., the customer experience) becomes much less than the sum of the individual, well-intentioned parts.

or even that they're bad employees. In fact, they are more than likely earnest, well-disposed people who are trying to do the right thing but are operating from a perspective that is different from yours.

The only place in your organization that has the perspective to truly appreciate the long-term value of the customer is at the top, where you're sitting. It's the only place where the positive impact of a commitment to killer customer care is clear and unambiguous. If your employees have been indifferent to customer care issues in the past, it's not necessarily that they are mediocre or second-rate. It's more likely that they are intelligent and conscientious but simply are not in a position to see the broad, long-term issues that foster an appreciation for the value of customer care.

Your responsibility as a manager is to communicate to your employees what the customer care picture looks like from *your* perspective. Beyond that, you'll need to be an evangelist—a dogged, determined evangelist—in your organization for the importance of killer customer care.

Prepare to Overcome Cultural Inertia with Persistence

You shouldn't be surprised or discouraged when you encounter organizational resistance to your new customer care initiatives. In fact, you should absolutely expect the inertia of your prior corporate culture to consistently cause each department in your organization to revert back to its own set of priorities and concerns. As an owner or senior manager, it will probably frustrate you that there is no switch you can flip to suddenly and permanently align your organization with your newly defined standards, particularly in an area that's as important as customer care. Unfortunately, such a magic bullet does not yet exist.

That doesn't mean, though, that a viable solution does not exist. Like so many other aspects of killer customer care, the answer to cultural inertia is not easy but it is simple. The only surefire way to overcome the resistance to change that's built into your organization is for you as a leader to be stubbornly persistent in your determination to direct and shape this change.

It's important to understand that most of your employees have been through this type of thing before, either at your company or with a previous employer. Some manager reads the latest management best-seller or attends a flashy seminar led by a charismatic speaker and gets fired up about a new management initiative. (Think back on your own experience over the years. You'll have to admit that there has been no shortage of trendy programs to emerge from the executive suite.) In most cases, these initiatives descend upon employees like a tornado. They appear suddenly, wreak havoc for a short period of time, then disappear as quickly as they appeared, leaving a mess in their wake. After going through one or two of these, your employees quickly figure out that their wisest course of action is to keep their heads down, lay low, do their jobs, and wait for the current "flavor of the month" to run its course.

Of course, this sort of reaction from your employees may be frustrating as you attempt to undertake something that is far more momentous than a "flavor of the month," but you'll have to admit that their reaction is not irrational and is even understandable. After all, they have no good reason to believe—until you give them one—that killer customer care is not going to join all those other programs in the dustbin of corporate history. The only way to effectively make your point is to do so consistently, no matter how long it takes.

Establish High Customer Care Standards

As we noted at the beginning of this chapter, killer customer care is something that won't work if it's undertaken half-heartedly or in moderate measures. If you want killer customer care to be a hallmark of your business, you've got to set high standards for yourself and your employees.

Incremental improvements in customer care are not enough to differentiate your business in the marketplace. It's not sufficient to just smooth out some of the rough edges. In a hypercompetitive marketplace, every one of your competitors is doing that. And a modest effort won't make your business memorable or remarkable in the eyes of your customers. That's one of the reasons why this book talks about "killer" customer care. To make a meaningful impression on your customers—the kind of impression that will deliver all of the benefits that we discussed in Chapter One—you'll need to achieve a level of customer care that elicits a "Wow!" reaction from your customers.

It is amazing and unfortunate that some "experts" do not understand how important it is for a business to deliver customer care that is above and beyond expectations. One popular book on the subject carries this admonition: "Going above and beyond has merit, of course. But why create an expectation you can't possibly meet on a regular basis?"

That's astonishingly bad advice. It's not just off the mark but is exactly the opposite approach to the one you ought to be taking. There is no value in aiming for a level of customer care that is less than the best you can possibly deliver. And if you are worried about the possibility of failing to meet your customers' expectations on a regular basis, Section III of this book will put your mind at ease.

Another reason why high standards are imperative is

Reshaping your corporate culture is equivalent to a long-term siege. Or—if you prefer a different metaphor—it is a marathon, as opposed to a sprint. Your employees are not trying to be deliberately obstinate. They're just reacting rationally to something new based on similar experiences they've had in the past.

Once you have shown a genuine, long-term commitment to a corporate culture based on killer customer care, they will get on board. It just takes sustained focus on your part. It's not easy, but it's simple.

And it takes time.

that they motivate your employees to a degree that more modest standards cannot. Killer customer care level standards make your employees feel as though they're undertaking something important. And, in fact, they are. Exceedingly high standards foster an atmosphere of teamwork and create a sense of pride in your organization, what used to be called esprit de corps.

You can get your employees jazzed by the prospect of delivering killer customer care, but you can't get them jazzed by the prospect of merely becoming marginally better than everyone else. Similarly, compare the motivational value of "We're going to deliver killer customer care," to the tiresome, "We're going to maximize shareholder value." Which do you think will energize your employees more?

Relentlessly Communicate the Killer Customer Care Gospel to Your Employees

Effectively shifting your company's culture is not an easy thing to accomplish. This is true even if your company is small and has only a few employees. If your company is a large one, making such a shift can be exponentially more challenging. However, as we've seen with other aspects of killer customer care, the key to your success may not necessarily be easy, but it is straightforward and simple.

Your company's senior managers must demonstrate to your employees over time that you're serious about establishing an environment for your customers that's based on the principles of killer customer care. It will take a fair amount of persistence for you to be successful. If persistence is going to be your strategy, then constant communication will be your most effective tactic. Your management team must communicate over and over again to your employees the value of killer customer care, the benefits of providing killer customer care, and the ways in which you expect this new strategy to be implemented.

Several effective communications techniques are discussed here.

Set a clear example. Most managers don't realize the degree to which their day-to-day behavior influences the behavior of their employees. You can preach about killer customer care as much as you'd like, but if an employee happens to see you or one of your managers handle a customer carelessly or make a cynical remark about a particular customer when that customer is out of earshot, then the months you spent evangelizing about customer care will have been squandered.

Don't miss an opportunity to evangelize. When you're trying to instill a new value into your corporate culture, it's got to be clear to everyone that this new value is a priority to you. That message doesn't come across if you spend your time in front of employees talking about something else. If killer customer care is your priority, then make it obvious and unmistakable by talking about it every chance you get. Will your employees get tired of hearing about it? Probably. Will they get the message? Absolutely. And, by the way, while you're working on getting this done, you need to be focused. Killer customer care can't be seen by employees as one of several company priorities because, as one management sage once observed, if you have several priorities, then you don't really have any priorities.

Use stories to make your point. Great leaders have understood for centuries that the best technique for communicating and motivating is through the use of stories. A

So you say you're running a business in the real world and have concerns besides customer care? Of course you do, and that's certainly understandable. The way to resolve this apparent contradiction is to link every one of your other ongoing issues to your overall goal of killer customer care.

For example, product quality can't go away because you'll never create a reaction of "Wow!" with second-rate products. It's an essential part of the program. The same thing is true of a plan to cut overhead costs. Your challenge is to frame your discussion of those subjects in a way that clearly relates back to the bigger concept of customer care.

well-placed story can be engaging and evocative. Instead of a dissertation on the value of customer care, use a story that illustrates how a real employee went out of his way to care for a real customer and, as a result, turned a one-time customer into a highly profitable repeat customer who also referred all of her family and friends.

Lectures are quickly forgotten, but a great story can become legendary within your company. And when you tell these stories, don't hesitate to *name names*. The employee who provided such terrific customer care deserves the public accolades. Telling a story about something a real employee did for a real customer is far more motivating than a story based on hypothetical situations.

Let's also look at a few pitfalls you'll want to avoid.

Don't second-guess good faith efforts to get it right. The formula for killer customer care is part science and part art. As your employees get used to operating in a brand new cultural environment, it's likely they're going to make mistakes no matter how thoroughly you think you've trained them. (At the very least, they'll do things differently than what you might have envisioned.) A sure-fire way to bring your killer customer care initiative to a screeching halt is to chastise well-intentioned employees for something that they did that's not quite what you wanted. If they get it right but don't quite succeed, then the first thing you should do is acknowledge and praise their efforts. Then, and only then, you can offer suggestions about how things might have been done differently.

Don't miss an opportunity to communicate directly with "the troops." If your company is relatively small, your employees probably have opportunities to regularly communicate directly with you. On the other hand, if you're a senior manager at a *Fortune* 500 company, then it might be

> *Just because something wasn't done exactly as you might have done it doesn't mean it wasn't done "right."*

relatively rare for front-line employees (i.e. the ones who are in contact with your customers every day) to have an opportunity to speak with you directly. Creating such opportunities, though, is a great way to highlight the importance of your message. When employees see that you are personally engaged in the issue of customer care—that customer care isn't something that's just written about in the company newsletter by a PR flack in an article that appears over your signature—they will be much more likely to embrace your attitude and make it their own. Take every opportunity you can to talk to the front-line people who talk to your customers every day. Allow them to see that killer customer care is genuinely important to you. And, while you're at it, listen to what they have to say. You might learn something, too.

Don't get sidetracked. There is no shortage of topics for you to discuss with your employees and middle managers. And when your company's transition to a culture of killer customer care is well on its way, there will be plenty of time to talk about all the other topics. In the meantime, though, you should try to emulate the one technique that the majority of our most effective political communicators use: stay on message. If someone wants to know about fixing inventory problems, don't get into a protracted discussion of inventory management. Instead, say something like, "While you're taking care of our customers face-to-face, better inventory management is one of the things that we'll be doing in the back office to support your efforts. Let's talk about how all of this fits together...." Of course, you'll sound as though everything you talk about comes back, over and over again, to customer care. But that's not a bad thing, really, because everything actually does.

Celebrate Customer Care Successes

One of the most powerful management tools at your disposal (and, inexplicably, the one that tends to be used least often by managers) is the power of praise. Although it might take a little bit of adjustment on your part, there's no doubt that you'll find the carrot to be far more effective than the stick when it comes to making a change in your company's corporate culture. Napoleon Bonaparte recognized this truth three centuries ago when he quipped that "a soldier will fight long and hard for a bit of colored ribbon." His observation applies to today's business environment as closely as it applied to the battlefields of the eighteenth century.

The key to turning this truism into a practical business tactic is to focus on catching your employees in the act of doing something right, then immediately and publicly praising them.

For example, if your business is a retail operation, you might observe one of your employees helping a mother whose hands are full with a couple of children. The employee escorts the mother out to her car and then loads her purchases into the trunk. You might stop that employee on the way back into the store and hand him or her a crisp $50 bill.

Immediacy is the most important element in this process. Beyond that, experience has demonstrated that cash in the form of brand new currency is significantly more motivating than a check. (No one is exactly sure why that's true, but it is.) The very next morning, you might single out your killer customer care ambassador in front of his or her colleagues for doing a terrific job.

It won't take too many incidents like that to make an indelible impression on all of your employees. Before long,

24 / CHAPTER 2

all of your employees will be competing for your attention by creating their own killer customer care moments.

Another complementary strategy for celebrating killer customer care is to inaugurate some sort of regular award to highlight employee achievements. Perhaps you might implement a monthly award along with a reserved parking spot for the employee who most consistently demonstrates the customer care principles that you're working to inculcate.

Finally, special rewards should be reserved for any instance of a customer taking the time and trouble to comment on care received from one of your employees.

A Final Word

One final word about setting the stage for your customer care program: Your employees won't take a customer care initiative seriously unless they are certain that you do. Most of the suggestions here emphasize a positive approach to changing your corporate culture. While the carrot is an effective motivator, that doesn't mean there's no place in your program for a corresponding stick.

Even a hint of cynicism among managers or employees will severely undermine all of your efforts. Such an attitude is toxic to an environment of killer customer care and cannot be tolerated or overlooked. If you find such an attitude in an employee or manager, it's important to take that individual to task as quickly and unambiguously as you possibly can.

Looking Ahead

Now that you have a grasp of the basics of setting the stage, let's turn our attention to the next step of the process: how to develop and implement an effective customer care plan.

There are several ways you could reward an employee showing killer customer care.
Good: *Pull a $50 bill out of your wallet and give it to your employee. That approach will certainly have a positive impact.*
Better: *Carry several envelopes in your jacket pocket or purse, each with a crisp, new $50 bill and a card that says, "Thanks for making our reputation for killer customer care a reality." This approach says you expect positive behavior from your employees and you're ready for it. It's a very powerful message.*

HOW TO DEVELOP YOUR OWN UNIQUE VISION OF KILLER CUSTOMER CARE

MAKING YOUR CUSTOMER CARE SPECIAL ◀

In more than twenty plus years of business consulting with hundreds of businesses, I have never—not even once—met an owner or manager who did not claim that his or her business was terrific at taking care of its customers. Clearly, experience and common sense dictate that not all of these businesses provided terrific customer care. In fact, the level of customer care that one could objectively observe at these businesses could be plotted on a standard bell curve. Some of the businesses were outstanding when it came to customer care, some were awful, and most fell somewhere in between.

Of course, all of the owners and managers I worked with had the best of intentions when it came to providing superior care for their customers, but very few of them had a specific vision to guide them in their efforts or a set of objective standards by which they could measure their success.

A Policy and Procedures Manual Is the Last Thing You Need

Let's get rid of the idea of trying to codify your customer care vision into something you can lay out in a manual or handbook. In spite of its intuitive appeal, a customer care handbook is almost always ineffective and more often than not can actually be an impediment to your efforts to instill a corporate culture based on the principle of killer customer care.

The fundamental shortcoming of a "policies and procedures" manual is that it can never anticipate all of the varied interactions your employees will have with your customers.

Moreover, when your employees are presented with a manual, they tend to interpret it literally, so that a handbook for customer care tends to keep your employees focused on the manual rather than on the customer. Attentiveness and responsiveness, both hallmarks of killer customer care, wind up taking a back seat to whatever is in the manual. Instead of supporting your goals, the manual becomes an impediment to two activities that are critical to delivering killer customer care: listening and thinking.

If your plan for killer customer care is going to be effective, it must focus on a broad vision, not the minutia of specific interactions. It ought to be more focused on outcomes than particular actions. Your approach to creating a cohesive customer care environment for your business should be more about making your employees consciously consider what they are doing than about memorizing something they read in a manual. Your customer care program needs to outline a clear set of basic principles your employees can use in making their decisions on a day-to-day, case-by-case basis.

And what happens, you might be wondering, if employees make mistakes? Go back to Chapter 2 and reread the part about not second-guessing your employees' good faith efforts. If your employees are actively thinking about customer care and what they might do to enhance your customers' experience, then you've accomplished the most important part of your task. Fine-tuning the details about how customer care principles translate into "real world" interactions is simple compared to engendering a practical, ongoing awareness of the importance of customer care.

Defining the Vision and Outlining the Principles

So, where does this vision come from? And how do you arrive at the principles that define your plan for providing killer customer care?

A great place to start is by developing a general idea of what you'd like to achieve, something I refer to as your "standards statement." In this document, you begin to formulate the high customer care standards referred to in Chapter 2. Don't worry about being too specific right now, although you can be as detailed as you'd like. Feel free to tinker and change this preliminary effort as your vision evolves. More than anything else, your objective right now is to set a tone for your subsequent efforts.

Here are some examples of standards statements that have been effective:

- Every customer who visits our store will be greeted courteously upon arrival and receive as much (or as little) sales assistance as they would like.
- If our customers are not 100 percent satisfied with their experience, they won't be expected to pay.
- We will deliver a fresh, hot pizza to our customer's door in thirty minutes or less, or their next pizza will be free.
- Every customer who enters our store should leave happy with the product and service they received.
- Every team member in our store is empowered to do "whatever it takes" to make sure every customer is happy with our products and service.

Deconstructing Your Competitors

Next, you'll want to spend some time conducting an assessment of what your competitors are doing with their customer care initiatives. You should make sure you're familiar with the customer care programs of each of your competitors. If you're not familiar with what they're doing, then it's critical you make the time to find out. And after your initial discoveries, make sure you make regular, periodic efforts to monitor the competition for any changes and/or improvements they make in customer care.

The purpose here is not to wind up with a rigorous, quantitative evaluation of your competitors' business practices. Instead, your objective is to collect customer care ideas and techniques that grab your attention and appeal to you at a visceral level. Finding ideas you're seeking will be something like the late Supreme Court Justice Potter Stewart's definition of obscenity: you'll definitely know them when you see them—even if you don't know exactly what you're looking for when you start. Is there anything your competitors are doing that makes you simply want to say "Wow!"? Then that's what you're looking for!

Identifying and adopting your competitors' best practices is an important step in developing your own approach to killer customer care, but it's not nearly enough. It's difficult to differentiate yourself in the marketplace by simply appropriating what others are doing. A thorough survey of your competitors' practices can ensure that your own customer care practices are not deficient or substandard in any important way. But if you're going to use killer customer care as a competitive weapon in the marketplace, then your competitors' best customer care practices will be only your starting point.

Beyond setting minimum standards, a review of what

If you're a student of marketing, you might notice that standards statements such as these shown in this chapter often become the basis of a business's USP or unique selling proposition. If you intend to explicitly position your business in the market based on customer care, then your efforts in creating a standards statement will do double duty as you simultaneously create your own USP.

Completing the Circuit

Consumer electronics retailer Circuit City found itself fighting for customers with two types of competitors: large-format retailers that carried a big selection of products at aggressive prices but offered little sales assistance; and online consumer electronics Web sites that offered detailed technical information and extensive research capability but made customers wait days for delivery.

Circuit City's response was to offer its customers the best of both approaches. It allowed them to research and compare products on its Web site and find out if the desired product was in stock at a local store. If so, customers could opt to purchase the product online, then pick it up at the store within hours. Or, customers could use Circuit City's Web site like a conventional consumer electronics Web site, making their purchases online and having them delivered to their home. This hybrid approach illustrates how Circuit City co-opted its competitors' best practices and combined them into its own unique killer customer care offering.

your competitors are doing may also suggest opportunities for you to pick several of their individual practices and combine them creatively.

You'll Only Think Outside the Box if You Step Outside the Box

One of my all-time favorite adages is this classic: "I don't know for sure who originally discovered water, but I guarantee it wasn't a fish!" The idea here is someone immersed in a situation or environment is unable to step back and look at that environment objectively. It often takes an outsider to really see what's going on.

This explains why the business practices of the major players in any given industry tend to closely synchronize over time. In the early days of an industry, there are no standards or benchmark performers. Every business is a maverick, and everyone is open to all sorts of new ideas and approaches. As a result, everyone innovates like crazy.

As the industry matures, however, the larger businesses in the industry begin to focus more and more on each other. Eventually, everyone in the industry looks more or less like everyone else. None of the major players wants to rock the boat because each one would rather protect his existing market share than gamble on something that's new and unproven.

This conformist mindset can impede innovative customer care practices as surely as it can stifle innovative products. If you're looking for ideas that will distinguish you from your competitors, spend some time looking at what companies in *other* industries are doing. That's where you're likely to find ideas and approaches that can be adapted and modified to meet the needs of your customers, ideas that will represent a genuine customer care breakthrough in your industry.

Consider the case of a young entrepreneur in the early days of the personal computer industry. At the time, the three industry heavyweights—IBM, Apple, and COMPAQ—were forcing their customers to buy their products from authorized retail dealers. All three had stringent requirements for their respective dealer networks, including detailed standards for the size and location of each retail location. Unfortunately, very few of those requirements had a positive impact on the quality of customer care. All but the largest business customers were often frustrated by the fact that they were not able to deal directly with the manufacturers.

Our nascent computer builder was very young, but he was smart enough to recognize an opportunity when he saw it. Rather than adopting the retail standard that was prevalent in the personal computer industry at that time, he looked outside of the industry for an idea that would allow him to alleviate customers' frustration with retail distribution channels and salespeople who were sometimes less than helpful and often less than knowledgeable. (A popular joke among buyers at the time was, "What's the difference between a used car salesperson and a computer salesperson? The used car salesperson knows when he's lying.")

This young entrepreneur's approach to killer customer care ignored the standards adopted by the personal computer industry and borrowed heavily from the catalog sales industry instead. Rather than building expensive retail outlets, he established a toll-free telephone number that allowed his customers to call his company directly to order personal computers. After the sale, if there were questions or problems, customers were able to deal with the company directly. His approach to dealing with customers wasn't original—after all, other industries had been using it for decades—but it was certainly unique in the personal computer industry. Customers responded enthusiastically to this appropriated strategy, and the young man's company, PCs Ltd., became quite successful.

You might be interested to know that the company's name was later changed to incorporate the name of its young founder, Michael Dell. The Dell Computer Corporation owes its success to a conscious decision by Michael Dell to not synchronize with established industry leaders. It borrowed its strategy for killer customer care from an entirely different industry.

Drilling Down a Level or Two

Although it's true that your customer care objectives will not be served by the creation of a policies and procedures manual, it's also true that a very broad vision of killer customer care is not going to provide enough direction for many of your employees. If they're going to have enough information and guidance to make informed decisions, then they're going to need you to fill in the broad outlines of your vision with a bit more detail. In order to do this, you'll want to consider which specific situations would benefit from more in-depth direction.

Examining the following questions will provide you an opportunity to determine where it would be useful to flesh out your broad vision of customer care with a greater level of detail.

What Are the Most Common Interactions We Have with Our Customers?

You'll certainly want to consider the Pareto Principle, more commonly known as the 80-20 Rule, as your vision for killer customer care evolves. Pareto's rule states that a small number of causes are responsible for a large percentage of effects, in a ratio of about 20:80. In a management context, the basic concept is that 20 percent of a business's effort generates 80 percent of that business's results. When it comes to your interactions with customers, the Pareto Principle may even understate reality. If you think about all of the ways in which your business and your employees interact with your customers, you'll find that a very small number of different situations account for the vast majority of interactions.

Make a list of your most common customer interactions. Do customers call your business? Do they walk in? Do they talk to salespeople on the sales floor? Do they normally interact with your business over the Internet? How are their questions answered after the sale? When you've identified your most common interactions (i.e. the ones that account for 80 percent or more of all your interactions), then you can establish specific principles that will govern each of those situations.

Are There Any Situations That Generate an Inordinate Amount of Complaints?

What are your customers complaining about? Again, if you take the time to analyze the specifics, you'll find that a few products/services/situations account for the majority of customer complaints. If you've never taken the time to do this, chances are you'll uncover results that are truly eye-opening. You'll learn a lot more about handling customer complaints in Chapter 20.

Obviously, if there's something your customers don't like that you're able to fix quickly or easily, by all means do so. For everything else, you'll want to outline the basic guidelines your employees should follow when an unhappy customer is identified.

Which Interactions Are Most Stressful for Our Customers? In Which Situations Are Our Customers Most Uncomfortable?

Apart from the kind of outright dissatisfaction that leads to customer complaints, your business interactions with customers may include situations that are stressful or uncomfortable. These situations can be easy for your employees to overlook in terms of their customer care implications. A patient waiting for dental work is one example of this kind of situation; a customer waiting for credit approval on a major purchase is another.

Are there any similar situations that regularly occur in your business? If so, do they tend to be ignored or dismissed by your employees as a natural or unavoidable part of your business process?

These types of situations are extraordinary opportunities to interject the quality of killer customer care into day-to-day customer interactions. They can be exactly the kind of occasion where attentiveness to customer care is most appreciated and noticed by your customers. What guidelines can you provide for your employees to minimize the stress your customers might feel when dealing with your business?

What Happens When a Customer Comes into Contact with Our Business for the First Time?

Your mother was right. You never get a second chance to make a first impression. This is the kind of phrase that copy editors regularly delete from books like this because it's too clichéd. Of course, the reason it's become such a cliché is that it's so true. The first contact your customer has with your business can set his or her expectations for the rest of the business relationship. It can also establish the tone for subsequent interactions. It is certainly a situation that deserves special attention as you define the principles that will guide your employees in delivering killer customer care.

What sorts of things can you do make this critical moment of contact as effective as possible? What do you want your employees saying or doing to let your customers know that yours is a special business, one that focuses on the quality of their customer experience in a unique and effective way?

Looking Ahead

As your own unique vision of killer customer care begins to evolve, there is one institutional skill that is singularly

If you find your business is taking customer stress for granted in certain situations, it's likely your competitors are doing the same. This provides you with a terrific opportunity to differentiate yourself.

important in making sure all of your customer care efforts are on track. That skill is listening to your customers effectively, and you will learn more about it in Chapter 4. If you don't do this well, it's almost impossible to sustain an effective customer care initiative. If you do it well, it's almost impossible to fail.

INSTITUTIONAL LISTENING: UNDERSTANDING AND ANTICIPATING YOUR CUSTOMERS' NEEDS

HOW TO LEARN WHAT YOUR CUSTOMERS WANT

Let's begin this chapter with a brief glimpse at two very different approaches two entrepreneurs took to listening to their customers. Then, we'll explore the implications that each approach has for your ability to deliver killer customer care.

Our first entrepreneur owned an upscale boutique that sold very chic, very fashionable women's clothing. Terry opened his first store in a trendy neighborhood with the intention of establishing a brand name and identity for his store in anticipation of creating a regional, then national, chain. Terry had a clear sense of how he wanted to position his chain in the marketplace and believed his selection of merchandise would be critical to his success. To his credit, he spent a great deal of time in the store, talking to customers and getting a feel for which fashions were in favor and which were not.

Two or three times a week, however, a customer would ask him if he carried lingerie. When asked, he would patiently explain that he did not and then recommend one or two stores in the area that did. Occasionally, however, he would find himself getting frustrated with his customers' apparently endless interest in lingerie. On more than one occasion, he was heard muttering something about his store being a clothing boutique, not a lingerie store. "If they want lingerie," he'd sigh, "they should go to Victoria's Secret." Apparently, they did. Terry never opened a second outlet, and his vision of a national chain of upscale shops died when he shut the doors on his only store two years after he'd opened.

A different approach to listening to customers is illustrated by Sonny, a software entrepreneur specializing in the specialty software market. The process of developing software can be risky and expensive, especially for a small company. Sonny's company, however, established an enviable track record over the years, almost never rolling out a poorly received product into the marketplace.

Sonny's secret for success was simple but audacious. Rather than investing money in speculative software development, he would engage a graphics design team to produce a mock-up package for the product he was thinking of introducing. He'd then take the "product" to the handful of distributors who dominated the industry. If he couldn't get enough orders to cover his development costs, the product idea was quietly shelved. Sonny would make some sort of plausible excuse to the distributors, cancel any outstanding orders for the never-finished software ("vaporware," in the parlance of the software industry), and move on to another more promising project.

So, which entrepreneur do you think was better positioned to provide his customers with killer customer care?

The Science (and Art) of Listening

The juxtaposition of these two examples hints at the value of listening to customers, especially when that listening is combined with a willingness to act on what you hear. The obvious lesson? You're in a much better position to deliver what your customers want if you actively and deliberately listen to what they have to say. But, like so many other basic principles, the ways in which this concept translates into "real world" business practices can be tricky.

In the two situations we just examined, the matter is probably a great deal simpler than it is in your business because, in each case, the listening environment is confined to what an individual entrepreneur could hear from his customers himself. Even if your business has only a handful of employees, your listening environment is probably significantly more complex than the ones Terry and Sonny had to negotiate. And if your business is even larger, or if it functions across multiple locations, then you're faced with a genuinely complex listening environment.

The term I use for effectively listening to customers in a business environment is *institutional listening*. It is a specific set of skills that, properly executed, will provide your company with the information it needs to consistently deliver on the promise of killer customer care. Six individual components make up *institutional listening*:

- Purposeful listening
- Active listening
- Capturing what's heard
- Aggregating what's captured
- Analyzing the aggregated information
- Acting on what you discover

Purposeful Listening

Remember that great old television series about the improbable but highly skilled detective? (It doesn't really matter which series you choose to remember. They all followed a pretty similar formula!) In it, the killer would betray his or her guilt with a slip of the tongue. The inadvertent admission would go unnoticed by just about everyone on the show. Everyone, that is, except the show's hero. He would instantly hone in on the mistake because he was listening with a purpose, listening with a specific outcome in mind. He knew what he was listening for. As a result, he would recognize the slip-up when he heard it.

That is the basic approach everyone in your organization needs to take when it comes to listening to your customers. When you train your employees in the principles of killer customer care, you'll need to make it clear that customers tend to behave like the villains on television—at least in one respect. They will almost never be explicit when it comes to telling you the things you need to know. Instead, that valuable nugget of information you're looking for is much more likely to be delivered as an offhand remark, a throw-away line that would almost certainly go unnoticed by your employees if they weren't listening with a purpose.

Your ultimate purpose in listening, of course, is to find out what killer customer care would look like to your customers. I am not suggesting that your employees' interactions with customers should turn into surveys or minifocus group sessions. (There's a place for both of those, however, as you'll discover in Chapter 24.) The strategy here is simply for your employees to listen purposefully, which means developing an awareness of comments or remarks made by your customers that touch on issues that impact your company's ability to deliver killer customer care.

Listening to Customers

Here is a list (by no means exhaustive) of the sorts of things that your employees should be listening for when they interact with customers:

- What are we already doing that they like?
- What would make it even better?
- What are we doing that they don't like?
- How would they do things differently?
- Are our competitors doing something better than we are?

- Is there something they wanted when they came here but didn't get before they left?
- Was there anything that surprised them?
- Was there anything that disappointed them?
- Was there anything that annoyed or frustrated them?

Remember, your customers will seldom come out and offer explicit answers to questions like these; getting the answers means listening "between the lines."

Active Listening

A skill closely related to purposeful listening is that of active listening. Purposeful listening is like being able to recognize a piece of treasure when you see it lying on the ground, even if it looks unremarkable to the untrained eye. Active listening is more like a willingness to dig a little to unearth the treasure when only a sliver is visible and the rest is buried under a pile of trash.

Most customers have come to believe their input is unwelcome and unwanted by the employees of the businesses they support. They believe this is true when they have any sort of observation or suggestion but perceive it to be especially true when they're unhappy about something. As a result, they are generally reluctant to be forthcoming when it comes to letting your employees know what they are thinking about your business and the way it operates. They may be candid—but they won't be *too* candid.

What your employees are likely to hear is just a hint of what's really on your customers' minds. This hint will

A typical exchange between an employee and a customer might start with a relatively innocuous question:

"How was everything today?"

"OK. Could have been better, I guess."

This sort of remark is made every day. Seldom does it get even a perfunctory follow up. Rarely does it get the kind of attention it deserves.

often come in the form of an offhand comment or a seemingly cryptic remark. If your employees are actively listening, they will not only recognize the hint when they hear it but will also make the effort to dig a bit deeper into the situation until they understand what's going on.

A passive listener goes through the motions, barely paying attention to what's been said. He is quite content to merely escape from the interaction unscathed and without any further responsibilities. If the customer doesn't seem to require additional attention, he's not going to get it.

An active listener, on the other hand, understands that the company's ability to provide killer customer care is built on the foundation of what he can learn from exchanges exactly like the one recorded here.

Active listening is an important tool for getting the information you need if you're going to create an atmosphere of killer customer care. It also communicates to your customer that the quality of his or her experience with your business is important to you and your employees, even when it comes to small things. It also says you don't take his or her business for granted.

Capturing What's Heard

Ah, here's where things get challenging. Even if your frontline employees do a terrific job at both purposeful and active listening, that's still not enough to make a difference. As a company, you are still left with the challenge of systematically delivering the information your employees have informally accumulated into the hands of the individuals who can use the information to create and maintain an environment of killer customer care.

The crucial aspect of effectively implementing this concept is that the transfer process needs to be systematic. After all, there's no trick to passing information around casually.

There's no particular value to it, either. A crisis might provide an opportunity for employees to let you know about customer concerns, but unfortunately, when that happens, it's usually too late to use the information effectively. Other management interactions with employees—ranging from performance reviews to water-cooler conversations—also facilitate this important communication. The problem is those things don't happen regularly or reliably.

If you're going to capture the information you need, you'll need to develop one or more dependable mechanisms for doing so. In order to be effective, those mechanisms must meet the following criteria,

First, they need to be readily available to each em-ployee who interacts with your customers. If you expect your employees to provide you with useful information about customers, then you need to make it as convenient as possible for them to do so. They should not have to wonder about how to let you know what's going on. The mechanisms you put into place should be obvious and readily available to your employees.

For example, if you're looking to collect information from employees who work outdoors, don't require them to find a desk with a computer in order to record customer information. Conversely, if an employee works at a desk with a computer, it wouldn't make sense to require her to stop what she is doing to fill out a paper-based form. Always provide your employees with a feedback mechanism that can be used conveniently from wherever they work.

Second, the time and effort required to capture information cannot be burdensome on the employee. Don't allow information collection to be an administrative chore. Whenever possible, provide forms (computer- or paper-based) with boxes to check or similar shortcuts that facili-

If your employee was an active listener, that exchange described above might go something like this:

"How was everything today?"

"OK. Could have been better, I guess."

"Oh? Was something wrong?"

"Well, it was no big deal."

"It doesn't have to be a big deal. Whatever affects your visit with us is important. If you could tell me what happened, I'd like to see if I can make it right."

While you're building feedback mechanisms for your employees to use, don't neglect to build some your customers can use, too. But, while direct feedback from your customers can be valuable because it is unfiltered, don't fall into the trap of giving it inordinate weight as you evaluate it. Customers who provide direct feedback are self-selected, and as a result, are not necessarily representative of your entire customer base.

tate easy data entry. If it takes too much time to capture the information, it won't get done.

Third, employees must not perceive that there's a penalty for delivering bad news. If employees tell you customers are complaining about some aspect of the products and services your company offers, don't chastise them for delivering bad news or argue with them about the merits of the customers' complaints. When an employee is telling you something you don't want to hear, he is doing you a favor. If your employees lose their motivation to tell you about a problem, then you might very well wind up being the only one who doesn't know when something is wrong.

Aggregating What's Captured

When feedback or input from your customers is captured, the next element of institutional listening should be to aggregate that information into a useful format. As a practical matter, this means getting the information entered into a computer.

If your employees are computer users for the most part, then this step is unnecessary because they'd likely log their input directly into the computer in the first place. Once it's entered, it will be a relatively easy matter to integrate it with whichever software tools you decide to use for analysis.

It's possible, however, that some of your employees do not use computers in their jobs. If that's the case, the information you need probably exists on paper and you'll need to establish a procedure for transferring that information into a computer system format. The most straightforward way of doing this is to assign the job to one or more of the people already doing clerical and administrative jobs for your company.

The important thing is to get all of the feedback and

input into a single place where it can be reviewed, analyzed, and translated into action steps that will move you toward your vision of killer customer care.

Analyzing the Aggregated Information

Clearly, this is the part of the process that is not only the most important but also the most difficult to codify. The analysis of the information you accumulate is part art and part science. It's a process influenced by your experience as a manager as well as your temperament and background.

For all of the subjectivity that the process necessarily entails, there are a few rules that can make it more straightforward. First of all, the information you accumulate can and should be divided into two categories: quantitative and qualitative.

Quantitative information consists of the feedback you receive that you're able to distill into numeric values. For example, if you're analyzing all of the negative feedback or complaints your business receives, you might break them down into categories. How many complaints are about your prices? How many are about your selection of merchandise? How many are about unsatisfactory interactions with your employees?

The specifics, of course, depend on your business. The governing principle, however, is that much of the feedback you receive can be broken down into categories that can be measured objectively. This quantitative feedback can then be formatted in a way that makes trends and anomalies as obvious as possible. In addition, quantified information can be graphed so that any patterns quickly become obvious.

The other category of information is qualitative. This refers to information that represents subjective feedback from customers. For example, a customer might tell one of your

*S*ome feedback might fall into both categories—quantitative and qualitative. If a customer mentions to an employee that your prices are higher than those at the XYZ Company ("XYZ always seems to have better prices than you around this time of year."), that feedback could be quantified as a complaint about price. The part of the remark that references a seasonal difference between you and your competitor could also be listed in the qualitative summary you review.

employees that your latest newspaper ad was confusing or misleading. This type of feedback should be summarized so you and your executive team members can review it.

There is no step-by-step, one-size-fits-all formula for gleaning insight from the information you accumulate. If you're like most businesses, though, chances are you're not doing this sort of analysis regularly. If that's the case, then just the process of looking at this information regularly will provide you with numerous insights into the kinds of policies, behaviors, and services your customers would consider to be their idea of killer customer care. The review and analysis of what your employees are hearing from your customers should be a regular, continual part of your management routine.

Acting on What You Discover

Finally, when you discover something in the course of your analysis, don't let your new insight linger as a merely academic curiosity. After all, the point of the analysis is not to engage in an academic exercise but to improve your customers' experience with your business, so you need to take action on what you learn.

As a practical matter, you should approach this as an iterative learning process. Use institutional listening to discover what your customers think, act on what you think you've heard, then listen some more to see how close you've come to getting it right.

Looking Ahead

Killer customer care is not necessarily what *you* think it is, and it's not what the rest of your industry thinks it is. Killer customer care is what your *customers* think it is. Contrary to conventional wisdom, the objective quality of your products or services does *not* determine your customers' perceptions. Rather, the determining factor is your ability to set and manage their expectations, a subject we'll explore in depth in Chapter 5.

*K*eep in mind that killer customer care is a moving target. No single tweak (or even major change) you can make can permanently align your business with the desires of your market. The marketplace in which you operate changes constantly. Your customers' priorities and sensibilities also change. Only through your mastery of institutional listening can you ensure your business will stay as closely aligned with your customers as possible.

SETTING AND MANAGING YOUR CUSTOMERS' EXPECTATIONS

MAKING YOUR CUSTOMER CARE SPECIAL

If a man can write a better book, preach a better sermon, or make a better mousetrap than his neighbor, though he build his house in the woods, the world will make a beaten path to his door.

Such was the state of the art of customer relations in 1871, at least as it was understood by Ralph Waldo Emerson, the author of that famous passage. Although the world has changed considerably since Emerson's day, the notion persists that there is a fixed relationship between the quality of the product or service you offer and the enthusiasm those products or services generate in your customers.

In reality, the relationship between those two values is far from fixed. Moreover, persistent misunderstandings about the relationship between quality and customer satisfaction cause endless confusion and countless mistakes on the part of businesses that want to provide killer customer care—but seem to consistently fall short despite their best efforts.

A Telling Scenario

The following hypothetical scenario will illustrate the issue a bit more clearly for you. I've told this story to hundreds of business owners and managers in dozens of workshops and seminars. The result I get is always the same.

Imagine you're in the market for a certain used car. You know exactly what you want—the exact make, model, and year of the car that's the object of your desire. As a careful shopper, you've researched your choice and have found the price range for your car of your choice is somewhere between $20,000 and $23,000, depending on mileage, condition, and other variables.

In the classified ads in your local newspaper you read a listing for a car that seems to fit your requirements exactly. You call the number and make an appointment to see the car, which is being sold privately. You consider yourself to be a fair negotiator and before you get to your appointment, you decide that if the car's in pristine condition (as the ad indicates it is), you'll shrewdly offer something like $17,500 and allow the seller to barter you up to $20,000, or even a bit more if the car is as nice as it sounds.

The sellers turn out to be an older couple, and the car turns out to be a real cream puff. It's in great condition; it's got low mileage; and it seems to have been meticulously maintained. You're determined to stick with your negotiating tact, however, so you make a showy inspection of the car, trying your best to convey the impression that you're aloof and dispassionate. After an appropriate amount of time kicking the tires and looking under the hood, you turn to the sellers and make your offer.

"It looks all right but not great. I'll give you $17,000 for it. "In your mind, you're preparing a counteroffer for their

anticipated rejection of your obviously lowball offer.

The couple confer with each other in a few perfunctory whispers, then turn to you and say, "That would be fine."

So, how would *you* react in that scenario? Chances are good that at least one of two different thoughts would come to mind:

I should have started lower. I could have gotten the car for a better price.

Something's wrong with this car.

When I describe this scenario in seminars, about 45 percent of the participants report their reaction included both of these responses, and 95 percent say they had one or the other.

What Happened?

Let's look at the objective reality here. You got exactly the car you wanted. It was well maintained, in good condition, and it had low mileage. And, as an added bonus, you found an opportunity to buy the car of your dreams for $3,000 less than you were prepared to pay, at least $3,000 less than what you knew to be the fair market value of the car. Any objective analysis of the situation would dictate you should have been delighted with the result of your negotiation.

However, the "real world" reaction an overwhelming majority of people have in this situation is distinct discomfort. Clearly, there's a dynamic at work here that is not strictly a function of the objective quality and value of the deal. Your understanding of this dynamic has profound implications for your business's ability to deliver killer customer care in interactions with customers.

The Delta Principle

The discomfort that most people feel in the used car scenario comes from a psychological mechanism I call the *Delta Principle*. This principle states that the quality of your customers' experiences is not a direct result of the objective quality of your products or services. Instead, customer satisfaction is a more a function of how closely your customers' experiences with your business conform with their expectations. As we saw in the used car scenario, the delta between expectations and reality don't have to be negative to produce a poor result—although that is, to be sure, a less common situation.

Customers' Expectations Are Not Always Obvious

The other significant lesson to be gleaned from that scenario is that there are usually many elements of an interaction—not just the obvious ones—that contribute to its quality. In the used car scenario, the price and condition of the car are the most obvious variables in evaluating the quality of the transaction. If those were the only elements,

Using the Delta Principle

The key to utilizing the Delta Principle effectively lies in framing your customers' expectations skillfully and then delivering on those expectations clearly and reliably. Of course, killer customer care means you can and should exceed the basic expectations your customers bring to the transaction (you'll find more on how to do that in Chapter 13), but you must do so in a way that is congruous with those expectations.

The used car scenario is something of an anomaly, but it is instructive nevertheless. As we've already seen, it demonstrates that a complete disconnect from a customer's expectation can lead to an unsatisfactory experience, even if the details of the disconnect are favorable to the customer.

however, then this scenario would produce a uniformly positive reaction, which it doesn't.

The buyer wanted something else from this transaction. He was probably not aware of it even after he realized the seller's response gave him a bad feeling. And it's even more important to note that the sellers obviously had no clue about this "hidden expectation" that the buyer brought to the transaction.

In addition to a quality car at a good price, the buyer in this scenario was looking for the satisfaction of "winning" in the negotiation. He had done his homework and taken the time to set the stage for the negotiation by putting on a show as he inspected the car. For this buyer, an important element of satisfaction was to be derived from his ability to prevail at the negotiating table. The quality of the interaction was diminished by the fact that he wasn't allowed to do so. Although it seems counterintuitive, this buyer's level of satisfaction might very likely have been enhanced if the seller had provided some stiff resistance in the negotiation. The buyer would have felt better about a somewhat higher price he'd worked for than he did about the lower price that came too easily.

When it comes to customer expectations, then, the three elements of delivering killer customer care are:

- Effectively setting expectations for your customers' experiences
- Understanding all of the expectations your customers bring to their transactions
- Delivering on your customers' expectations explicitly

Effectively Setting Expectations for Your Customers' Experiences

The process of setting customer expectations begins with the very first element of contact. Often, this is an advertisement or some sort of marketing piece. Occasionally, it is a news item or other public relations-generated mention of your company, product, or service in the news media. Unlike referrals, these are communication vehicles over which you have a considerable, or even total, amount of control.

The messages that are contained in these communications are almost always crafted with the objective of driving customers to your business—and most often they're targeted toward new customers. But these communications can sometimes do long-term damage if they set unrealistic or inappropriate expectations. They might be successful in getting customers into your business, but in doing so, they can inadvertently undermine your ability to generate an experience that satisfies the new customer.

Such a result is unnecessary. A little more thought, along with an understanding of the Delta Principle, will allow you to craft a highly effective advertising/marketing message that supports, rather than undermines, your long-term killer customer care objectives. When it's time to craft an advertising, marketing, or public relations message for your company, consider the questions discussed below.

Is this communication congruent with my standards statement? In Chapter 3, we discussed the creation of a standards statement for your business that communicates your particular vision of customer care. Every marketing communication you create should reflect the values of that statement, or at the very least, not contradict them.

Market on Customer Care

If your standards statement is predicated on exceptional customer care, then a marketing message emphasizing aggressive pricing will attract customers who are looking for something different from what you're offering. Those customers' expectations, are unlikely to ever be met. Conversely, if your standards statement positions you as the value leader in your marketplace, then a marketing message that emphasizes customer service will create a comparable problem. Being the low-cost provider in your market seldom provides enough available margin to support an extensive customer service infrastructure.

Remember, the point here is not to argue for the relative merits of either approach. The point is that the expectations you've created for your customers with your advertising and/or marketing message should match the experience they actually have with your business when they get there.

Am I explicitly promising anything in this communication? Obviously, every promise you make in an advertisement creates a clear expectation on the part of your customer. When you do this, two critical elements are involved in making certain your marketing message hasn't become counterproductive by the time your customer leaves your business.

The first is to make certain everyone in your organization is aware of everything being promised. If a customer has to spend even a few minutes waiting for someone who's familiar with your business's current promotion, it can significantly diminish the quality of that customer's experience. The second fundamental principle in fulfilling your marketing promises is to do so as quickly as possible, without the customer having to ask for what you have promised. When you are forthcoming with whatever it is that your customer expects, your credibility shoots up while your customer's anxiety level drops down.

If you can execute these two techniques flawlessly, explicit promises are a highly effective tactic for setting customer expectations.

Am I implicitly promising anything in this communication? Marketing and advertising often can convey distinct impressions to customers without actually making any overt commitments. This is a natural part of the process of romancing your company's products and services. Customers automatically "discount" what they see and hear to a certain extent, but there can be times when your marketing message conveys an impression so disconnected from the reality of doing business with your company that it creates a real problem for you downstream.

If your television ads depict all of your salespeople as young, thin, and attractive, but they're not, that is an impression that could plausibly be called artistic license. On the other hand, if you run a print ad that gives the impression your company offers same-day service when your most aggressive turn-around time is three or four business days, then you are positioning your customer for disappointment and creating a situation that will not allow you to offer killer customer care.

Understanding All of the Expectations Your Customers Bring to Their Transactions

As we saw in the used car scenario, customers bring many different kinds of expectations to a transaction. For almost every business, a whole set of these unconscious or "hidden" expectations affect the quality of its customers' experiences. If you focus only on the most explicit expectations, then your customers' experiences will almost certainly be much less satisfying than possible. Sure, you must address your customers' primary expectations, but you should also be tenaciously trying to understand *all* of your customers' expectations—especially the hidden ones—and then exploring ways to address them all.

Don't Create Discord

Here's a hint: one common thread that runs through the unconscious expectations of most customers is that their experience with your business be congruous. No single aspect of the experience should seem discordant with the rest.

Consider, as an example, the prospect of a new, deep-discount retailer that, in its advertising and marketing, positions itself as having prices competitive with, say, Sam's Club. What kind of reaction do you think a customer might have if she visited the retailer and found a store with meticulous aisles and displays, a business merchandised more like Nordstrom's than Costco?

Chances are that customer would never feel as though she were getting the best prices, regardless of how this retailer's prices objectively stacked up against the competition. That's because the merchandising of the store does not conform with the customer's unconscious expectations.

Customers are seldom entirely satisfied with a transactional business relationship. In addition to your product or service, your customer will sometimes be looking for a friend and confidant; sometimes, he will be seeking an authority figure, even a surrogate parent; and sometimes your customer will be looking for some kind of status or validation. In any event, your ability to deliver killer customer care often depends on how well you can identify and address these ancillary expectations.

Delivering on Your Customers' Expectations Explicitly

In many ways, the procedure for setting and managing your customers' expectations follows the basic pattern of the three-part adage often shared with would-be speechmakers and essayists:

1. Tell them what you're going to tell them.
2. Tell them.
3. Tell them what you've told them.

It's that last part of the process that can make the difference between failure and success when it comes to your customers' perceptions of whether or not their expectations have been met. Often, the best way to ensure customers feel their expectations have been addressed is to simply tell them they have.

This is particularly true when specific representations were made in your advertising and marketing. Let's say you ran a newspaper ad promising a 50 percent discount on the purchase of a certain brand of widget. If you automatically and unceremoniously rang up the widget at the cash register with the discounted price, you fulfilled the terms and conditions of your promise, but it's likely you didn't address your customers' expectations. In fact, if you've ever tried that approach, your cashiers were almost certainly accosted by several customers who wanted to know if they were being charged the right price.

A better approach would be to program your point-of-sale software to show the original price of the widget along with the discount promised in your ad. In this way, you explicitly demonstrate to your customers that you've met their expectations.

Albertson's, the large supermarket chain, is one example of an organization that doesn't leave the customer's perception to chance. The chain's point-of-sale software automatically notes the regular price of an item, then makes appropriate deductions for sales pricing or other discounts on an item-by-item basis. Then, when the receipt is printed out, it not only specifies the total price of the order but also includes an item on the receipt indicating exactly how much money was saved on that particular order. This approach explicitly demonstrates to customers that their expectations for saving money are met with each and every visit to the store.

Albertson's takes this principle one step farther, however, into the realm of killer customer care by training each of the chain's cashiers to follow a specific technique when handing a receipt to a customer. Instead of just putting the receipt in a bag somewhere with the groceries, the cashier takes the receipt and circles the amount of money saved by the customer with a red pen. Then, the cashier hands the receipt to the customer and says, "You saved $xx on your visit to Albertson's today. Thank you and please come again."

Every customer who buys something leaves with a clear and explicit understanding that his or her expectation of saving some money has been met. The customer's perception of savings is met and managed because the store makes those savings obvious.

Whenever you do something to meet your customers' expectations, don't leave it to chance that they will realize what you've done. Follow through with the final piece of the process by delivering on your customers' expectations explicitly.

Looking Ahead

For most businesses, killer customer care requires more than just a few people working to address customer expectations. For your business to perform at its highest level, it requires that everyone function as part of a team. But teamwork doesn't happen by accident. In the next chapter, we'll explore specific techniques for encouraging your employees to function effectively as members of a team that shares your goals and values.

TEAMWORK DOESN'T HAPPEN BY ACCIDENT

WORKING TOGETHER FOR YOUR CUSTOMERS ◀

Teamwork is a genuine pleasure to watch, whether it's on a field or in an office. The principles involved in making teamwork happen are the same in both settings: it always looks a lot easier than it really is; it always takes a great deal of behind the scenes work to make it happen; and when it does happen, it always means pride, ego, and selfishness have been set aside in favor of a larger, more compelling vision.

Unfortunately, in the world of business, it is often easier to find examples of management obstructing teamwork than supporting it. Even more discouraging is the fact that this management obstruction is usually not an isolated incident or a thoughtless episode. Instead, teamwork is frequently undermined (or even actually discouraged) by structural or systemic impediments that unthinking managers create for their own convenience.

If your business aspires to outstanding levels of customer satisfaction, then you first need to identify the artificial obstacles that interfere with the level of teamwork required to achieve killer customer care.

Creating Harmony for Customers

Why is teamwork so important to killer customer care? Because customers view your business as a single unified entity. They are looking for a specific result and a high level of performance relative to their expectations and couldn't care less about your company's internal politics or organization. If you're going to achieve the kind of end-to-end proficiency that constitutes killer customer care, then every member of your team needs to be working toward the same goals.

The activities of your employees need to be coordinated—even orchestrated—to deliver the results you want. When they don't work together, the outcome is as obvious (and unsettling) as an orchestra member playing from the wrong score in the middle of a symphony.

Structural Impediments to Teamwork

Your employees are not inherently averse to working together as a team. On the other hand, they're not inherently disposed to do so, either. The extent to which they will or will not be willing to perform together as members of a team depends largely on their work environment. Later in this chapter, we'll look at some specific techniques for fostering teamwork. But your fundamental priority as a manager must be to adhere to advice found in the famous first words of the physician's Hippocratic Oath: *First, do no harm.*

Translating that advice into a set of real-world tactics means ridding your business of any structural impediments that undermine or discourage teamwork. Thoughtless policies in three areas can inadvertently put teamwork-killing structures in place:

- Ill-conceived compensation plans
- Inflexible organizational structures
- Poorly designed processes

Ill-conceived Compensation Plans

The basic principle here was outlined years ago by psychologist Michael LeBeouf in a book called *The Greatest Management Principle*. In it, he argued that employees tend to do those things they are paid or rewarded to do, an observation that is both simple and profound. Many management challenges occur as a result of not thinking through how this principle, which seems self-evident at first glance, applies in real-world situations.

Consider how Lebouf's principle might work in a retail environment that conducts high-ticket sales (high-end electronics or appliances, for example). In most stores, a particular salesperson is likely to be unavailable during most of the store's working hours. That salesperson is probably only "on the floor" for a little more than half of the ninety-something hours the store is open in any given week, and when he or she is at work, most of that time ostensibly is occupied helping customers. Let's suppose this store's salespeople work exclusively (or even primarily) on straight sales commission, not an uncommon circumstance in the high-ticket sales environment.

Now, let's imagine a customer who made a recent purchase is visiting the store with a question or problem. If the salesperson who made the original sale is not available,

Applying Labeouf's Principle

A very common and very straightforward example of failure to apply Lebeouf's principle is summed up in a quip made by the owner of a computer retail outlet. Referring to "spiffs," the cash payments often made by manufacturers to salespeople who sell a great deal of equipment in a designated period of time, this owner lamented the fact that manufacturers often give lip service to customer care but seldom reward it. "Just once," he said, "I'd like to see them spiff customer satisfaction."

He was right, of course. It's one thing to talk about customer care, but if you're actively rewarding sales volumes, it shouldn't be too difficult to predict where your salespeople are going to put their attention and effort.

how likely is it that this customer is going to receive the kind of treatment and attention that rises to the level of killer customer care? If we're going to be realistic and candid, the fact is it isn't likely at all. This sales compensation system is optimized for revenue-generation not customer care. Without compensation elements designed to address customer-care issues, this store has a structural impediment to killer customer care.

A variation of the same problem is found in businesses that offer incentive-based compensation to salespeople but no one else in the organization. This type of disparity tends to foster resentment among employees who do not have the opportunity to increase their compensation, and that resentment can manifest itself in substandard care for customers. These employees frequently take the attitude that their colleagues who are getting compensated to do so should be the ones to take care of customer concerns or problems. Is that a reasonable or justifiable attitude? Probably not, but it's not uncommon. The point here is that the structure of a business's compensation plan can contribute to teamwork problems that might have been avoided with a plan that's more closely aligned with the company's customer care objectives.

Inflexible Organizational Structures

You've probably heard the adage, "The map is not the territory." Any artificial representation of reality such as a map is useful only within certain specific parameters and will always vary from the reality it represents in significant, although not always readily apparent, ways. Ultimately, it is the territory (reality) that's important, not the map.

Along these lines, a business has a number of good reasons to create artificial representations of its organizational structure. Those representations quickly and simply convey lots of information about how the company works. They show how information flows through a company. They provide a framework for understanding how things get done and how decisions are made.

But, like any other map, they can become dangerous if they're used improperly, especially if the artificial representation is given a significance that transcends the underlying business reality. Organization structures can undermine teamwork in two significant ways. The first is when they create an arrangement that makes it difficult for employees from different departments to work together to address customer needs or concerns.

A second, related way organizational structures impede the pursuit of killer customer care is when they are treated as though they're more important than the "on the

Signs of Inflexibility

Some telltale signs of an inflexible organizational structure are:

- Employees have difficulty getting information they need to help customers.
- Direct communication between employees in two or more departments is being discouraged.
- Inordinate amounts of time are spent on "turf" issues.
- Customer problems get "handed off" regularly.
- Interdepartmental meetings on customer-related matters do not occur.

- Political struggles between department heads are overt.

In any of these situations, there is a danger of instilling what I call "corporate myopia," a situation in which each department comes to view the world solely in terms of its own concerns. In turn, employees of each department are encouraged to focus their attention on their own priorities, leaving other departments to do the same. Problems tend to get pigeon-holed in a specific department, even in cases where responsibilities (as well as potential solutions) overlap from one part of the organization to another.

ground" reality of attending to customers. The danger is that the organization structure itself comes to be thought of as more important than focusing on customer-care issues. Employees of businesses that suffer from this mindset are far more concerned with doing things "by the book" than with solving customer problems. Problems and concerns are handled in a manner that is "tidy" rather than one that is expeditious. The result is often a situation in which every employee in a given chain of events does what he or she is "supposed" to do, but the end result is one that's unsatisfactory for the customer.

Poorly Designed Processes

Most of what happens in business takes place in the context of a "process," a series of steps designed to create a certain result. Sometimes, a business's processes are well thought out and formally defined; other times, they're more informal. In either case, employees usually have an understanding of how things are supposed to get done, and they try to function within the boundaries of the company's existing processes.

Unfortunately, these existing processes are often at odds with the requirements of killer customer care. That's what happens when they are designed for the convenience of people or departments within a company, not for the convenience of customers.

An example of a process that interferes with killer customer care might be a merchandise return policy designed by someone in operations focused primarily on whether or not a returned item might be eligible for credit from the manufacturer, not on the impact the process would have on the customer. The resulting process would surely result in fewer returns overall, as well as a higher percentage of returns being eligible for return credit—a successful outcome in the view of the operations department.

But a broader perspective would likely reveal the development of a chronically adversarial relationship between sales and operations, undermining any chance of the two departments working together smoothly as a team.

Five Proven Strategies for Promoting Effective Teamwork

Now that we've examined the ways in which teamwork gets undermined, let's turn our attention to some specific things you can do to make sure your employees are working together like a championship football team or a world-class ballet company. Great business teams consistently employ five specific strategies that will make your road to superior customer care performance immeasurably easier if you incorporate them into your overall corporate action plan. The five strategies to employ are:

- Relentlessly focus your employees on "the big picture"
- Develop compensation structures that are closely aligned with team goals
- Use each individual's particular skills and strengths appropriately
- Insist on high standards of performance
- Lavishly celebrate team success

Relentlessly Focus Your Employees on "the Big Picture"

In most organizations, all but the most senior positions are compartmentalized arrangements, with a primarily internal focus. This leads to an almost inevitable inclination to gauge one's effectiveness according to very narrowly defined criteria (something we discussed in greater detail in Chapter 2). If the organization is structured properly, this internal focus isn't a big problem in most situations because department goals usually support larger organizational objectives.

But even in the most carefully structured environments, situations can occur in which it's appropriate for individual or departmental objectives to be subordinate to the more global corporate objective of killer customer care. When those situations occur, it's important for employees to know exactly what the company's larger priorities are and to understand there are no penalties for any actions or decisions that temporarily overlook individual or departmental priorities in favor of corporate objectives.

Consider the fact that, over the past thirty years, the individual home run champion in any given year has never been on the winning World Series team. Why does the player with the game's best offensive weapon so seldom achieve a championship? Many experts believe that in today's free-agent baseball environment, sluggers are often reluctant to give up individual statistics in favor of strategies that might be more beneficial to the team.

Moreover, most managers can't or won't try to refocus the hitting star on the team's objectives. As a result, when a slugger comes to bat late in the game with no outs and a man on first, he takes his chances swinging for the fences rather than making the sacrifice fly that could advance the runner to second base. Over the course of a season, this may add a few homers to his total, but it also could cost his team several games.

Similarly, an employee who believes her productivity is judged by her shelf-stocking output and nothing else might be more inclined to answer a customer's question curtly than interrupt what she's doing to give the customer more attention and a more complete answer.

In both of these cases, the team's performance would be improved by a consistent, congruent focus on *team* objectives on the part of management. In the case of the employee stocking shelves, your consistent message should be that the first priority of *every employee* is to take care of customers. Once that message is conveyed, management needs to make certain its behavior is congruent with the message. In this instance, that would be accomplished by not penalizing an employee who frequently interrupts what he or she is doing to attend to a customer's immediate needs.

Develop Compensation Structures That Are Closely Aligned with Team Goals

The basic premise that ought to guide the design of an effective compensation plan is simple: if you want your employees to act together as a team, then you should create a compensation system that rewards them—at least in part—based on team performance. Of course, there is a place for compensation that rewards individual effort, but most compensation structures (especially those found in the sales department) are overly oriented toward individual rewards. These plans would be more effective if they also rewarded team achievement.

A team-oriented compensation structure rewards cooperation and eliminates any unintentional incentives for individual employees to subordinate the customer's interest in favor of their own. If you do this properly, a customer with a problem or question will never again hear a salesperson say "Wait here and I'll get Sarah. She's the one who took care of you when you bought this." Instead, every salesperson (and every other employee, for that matter) will be attentive to the customer's needs because they are part of a team that exists for the express purpose of providing killer customer care.

A related issue is that the performance of non-sales employees is enhanced when at least some of their compensation is based on the overall team's performance. The chasm that exists in many companies between the sales department and everyone else is reduced, if not entirely eliminated, when performance-based incentives are available to all.

Use Each Individual's Particular Skills and Strengths Appropriately

Your employees are unique individuals with their own particular strengths and weaknesses. One of your challenges as a team-builder and coach is to make sure that each team member is being utilized appropriately and effectively. You may occasionally need to adjust your game plan a bit, but

Sometimes It's Good to Be "New School"

Until 1983, Don Shula, the Hall of Fame coach of the Miami Dolphins, was as traditional and conservative as any coach in the National Football League. Like most "old school" coaches, he was intent on establishing a running game and using the pass sparingly and strategically. This traditionalist approach had produced a great deal of success for Shula, including two Super Bowl crowns with the Dolphins and distinction of being the coach of the only NFL team to have an undefeated season. In 1983, however, Shula found himself coaching a young quarterback who possessed one of the most extraordinary arms that the NFL had ever seen, Dan Marino.

Shula could have insisted that Marino adapt himself to the team's conservative game plan. Certainly no one would have questioned the judgment of a coach with two Super Bowl rings. But Shula understood that Marino brought a unique set of skills to his position and was flexible enough to adjust his coaching to take advantage of Marino's special talent.

the payoff is a team that functions more smoothly because its members are more comfortable with their respective assignments.

Insist on High Standards of Performance

Tom Peters once famously speculated on the motivational value of an imaginary corporate slogan, "We're no worse than anyone else!" As Peters rightly pointed out, that level of ambition is not going to inspire anyone nor will it serve as the rallying point for a great team effort.

If you want to encourage the kind of teamwork that produces killer customer care, you're going to need a more inspirational goal with high standards and high expectations.

The manager of a Toyota dealership in Florida knew the value of an inspirational goal when he described the standard of achievement he expected from his employees. After a customer makes a purchase or visits the dealer's service department, the factory contacts that customer and asks for an evaluation of the dealer. The evaluation is conducted on a scale of one to five, with one being the lowest and five being the highest. At this particular dealership, the manager's standards are both clear and ambitious. "As far as I'm concerned, five is the only acceptable score for us. Scoring four is not merely disappointing, it's an abject failure."

This manager provides his team with standards that are unambiguous and quantifiable. And they are high. High enough to get his employees focused and high enough to produce a level of performance at his dealership that can only be described as killer customer care.

Lavishly Celebrate Team Success

Psychologists call it positive reinforcement. It is the active, open, public lauding of your team members' achievements.

Chances are you already use this management tool extensively in certain areas of your business. Publicly praising salespeople who meet and exceed their sales quotas is a fairly standard practice among companies of all sizes and in all different industries.

But this practice need not be limited to sales achievement. It works just as well in reinforcing all sorts of positive behaviors. If teamwork is a behavior you want to encourage, then, lavish praise on your employees when you catch them working together as a team.

When possible, the most effective use of this technique is to catch employees in a good act and praise them for what they're doing right on the spot. Even when that kind of immediacy is not possible, your consistent and explicit commendation of team-oriented behavior will get your employees' attention. Over time, it will translate into more of the teamwork-oriented behavior you're trying to encourage.

Looking Ahead

Even after you've gotten everyone working together as a team, your job as a manager and coach isn't finished. In fact, you're just getting ready to start working on some of the fundamentals of killer customer care. In the next chapter, you'll learn about the principles involved in dealing effectively with customers in a very important, very common situation. In Chapter 7, we'll explore the dynamic of face-to-face customer contact.

UNLEASHING THE DYNAMICS OF FACE-TO-FACE CONTACT

GETTING PERSONAL SHOWS YOU CARE ◀

A classic motivational story from years ago told of a man who had devoted his life to finding diamonds in an old abandoned mine he'd purchased. Year after year, he dug relentlessly without finding anything, finally giving up and living out the rest of his days as a broken and defeated man. Only after his death, according to the story, was it discovered that he had stopped digging just a foot or two short of one of the largest diamond finds of the era.

Although this story is almost certainly apocryphal, it serves as an instructive parable about how people can expend a tremendous amount of effort in an important undertaking and not reap any rewards because they didn't take that small, extra step that would have completed the job.

In many ways, the story describes the kind of exasperating behavior many companies exhibit in the marketplace every day. These underachieving companies spend tremendous amounts of money and expend enormous effort to convince prospects to visit their stores or sales offices. Ostensibly, they do this in an attempt to create ongoing, repeat customers. Amazingly, though, after they've successfully completed the most difficult part of the process, these companies fail to execute the relatively easy steps required to finish the job. They fail in the all-important area of face-to-face interactions with customers.

The sad part is that following a few straightforward rules would make all the difference in the world. That's why this chapter is so important. It contains ten simple steps you can take to make sure all of your face-to-face customer interactions are positive for your customer and effective for you. Following these rules isn't expensive, and it doesn't require a superhuman effort. It just requires a willingness to focus on this issue and a determination to consistently execute a simple game plan. If you do that, your customer interactions will reach the level of killer customer care and significantly differentiate your company in your marketplace.

There are ten rules for achieving killer customer care in all of your face-to-face interactions with customers.

1. Greet the customer in a timely manner.
2. Smile!
3. Tell the customer what to expect/what's going on.
4. Look your customer in the eye.
5. Follow the customer's lead.
6. Be available.
7. Live customer trumps the telephone
8. Stay focused on the customer.
9. Capture customer information for follow-up contact.

10. Prepare for all of the most likely scenarios.

We'll examine each of these rules in detail. As we do, you'll see just how simple it can be to take your business's face-to-face interactions with customers to an entirely new level.

One: Greet the Customer in a Timely Manner

The first few minutes of your customer's visit can often set the tone for everything that follows. It's possible to recover from a misstep at this early stage of interaction, but why start out with a strike or two against you when getting it right is so easy?

There are two elements to an effective greeting. The first is to make sure it happens in a timely manner. Understand that "timely" does not mean "hurriedly." Customers will often feel uncomfortable when they feel they've been pounced on as soon as they arrive at your place of business. A timely greeting means giving your customers a moment or two to get their bearings.

The other element of an effective greeting is the content of the greeting itself, the specific words your employees use to welcome a customer to your place of business. One obvious variable has to do with whether or not your employee recognizes a customer from a previous visit. If so, that recognition should be clearly communicated with something simple and straightforward like "Welcome back."

Beyond that, the specific wording you'll want your employees to use to achieve killer customer care will depend on a few variables. For starters, let's agree that "Can I help you?" is not going to be effective under any circumstances. It's trite, clichéd, and virtually begs for the conversation-stopping answer "No thanks, I'm just looking around."

> *E*ffective timing is part art and part science, but a serviceable rule of thumb is to give your customers more time before greeting them if your place of business tends to produce a sensory overload. That type of reaction occurs if the environment is large, crowded, or if there's a lot of visual stimulation. Conversely, if your place of business is small and spare, your customers will need less time to get acclimated, so you should offer a greeting sooner.

Instead, craft a greeting that is pleasant, friendly, upbeat (although if you happen to be in the funeral business, let your own best judgment prevail!), and reflects the probable mindset your customer brings. If your business is likely to be familiar to your customer—a dry cleaner or convenience store, for example—then your greeting merely needs to acknowledge the customer's arrival and let him or her know that help is available if needed. In such a situation, you'll want to allow the customer to feel in control.

On the other hand, perhaps your business is likely to be less familiar to a visiting customer. Businesses in this category are ones a customer patronizes infrequently. A real estate business specializing in residential sales would be an example of this type of business because most people buy a house only once or twice in their lives. Also in this category are businesses that sell or distribute a familiar product or service in an innovative fashion. (The original warehouse outlet stores would have been examples of this when they first appeared on the retailing scene more than a decade ago.) If your business falls into this category, then the objective of your greeting should go beyond acknowledging the customer's presence and aim to put the customer at ease and make him or her comfortable as quickly as possible.

A great start is to welcome the customer, then ask, "Have you ever been to one of our stores/offices before?" This greeting lets customers know that it's OK to be unfamiliar with the surroundings and that they won't be left to wander around aimlessly. Once they acknowledge that they've not visited your business previously, then you can let them know about how you do business and what they can expect.

Two: Smile!

It's tempting to gloss over this point or address it in a cursory way when you're training employees, but doing that would be a big mistake. A smile lowers your customers' resistance and stress levels. It puts them at ease and facilitates almost any imaginable kind of interaction you might have (with the possible exception of the aforementioned funeral scenario!).

The reaction your customers have to being greeted with a smile is immediate, reflexive, visceral—and overwhelmingly positive. If that's the case, then why isn't smiling an automatic part of every employee's repertoire? Like so many other aspects of killer customer care, the simple truth is that a lack of a smile is almost always a matter of neglect. Often, employers don't realize the importance of smiling because they just don't think about it. Many times, it never occurs to them to include something so fundamental in their employee training. They assume employees instinctively understand the value of a smile. Incredibly, it is occasionally the case that employers feel it's unprofessional or even intrusive to address the fundamentals of demeanor in employee training.

The truth is that smiling is seldom a natural element of an employee's style of interaction with customers. Many

You're on Stage!

A useful way to think about the art of putting on a smile—for both you and your employees—is to imagine that every interaction with customers is a stage performance. Thought of that way, the object of the interaction is obviously not to "be yourself." Instead, it's to play a role. In this case, it's a role that's largely unscripted, but it's still an artificial behavior that's designed to work in a specific situation, a classic improvisation.

Entertainment companies like Disney have a natural advantage when it comes to this approach. Disney dresses many of its employees in costumes and refers to all of them as "cast members." When you're a cast member, it's not hard to remember to "act" a particular way all of the time. It's a very effective metaphor, one that you might want to modify and appropriate for your employees.

people feel like grinning idiots the first time or two they undertake a deliberate attempt to smile. Therefore, like every other aspects of employee behavior, smiling should be addressed explicitly in training and monitored periodically.

You can anticipate a certain amount of "push back" from some of your employees. They'll tell you that they don't feel like smiling and that customers will sense their smiles are insincere and be put off by that. The response to that argument is simple and straightforward: customers always prefer insincere cheerfulness to sincere surliness!

The atmosphere of your entire business will change as employees acquire the habit of smiling. By the way, don't be surprised if your employees start enjoying their work a bit more when they're smiling. Think of it as an ancillary benefit. Killer customer care is not incompatible with outstanding employee morale. Just the opposite is much more likely to be true.

Three: Tell the Customer What to Expect/What's Going on

As we saw in Chapter 5, an important element of killer customer care is your ability to appropriately set and manage your customers' expectations. Whereas this is a principle that should pervade every aspect of your customer relationships—beginning with your marketing and advertising messages—it is something that is particularly effective when it's done face-to-face.

Consumer businesses tend to do this more regularly than organizations engaged in business-to-business commerce, which is an unfortunate oversight on the part of companies that engage in business-to-business transactions. A good deal of miscommunication and frustration could be avoided if businesses acquired the habit of explaining to their fellow business customers exactly how their processes and procedures work.

Here are a few examples of the information you might want to share with your customers about what they can expect when dealing with you.

- How long the process/transaction is going to take
- A list of Frequently Asked Questions (along with their answers, of course!)
- Specific steps that need to take place for the transaction to be completed
- Various options available to the customer
- The customer's recourse if he or she is unhappy
- A list of contacts at your organization

A confident, anxiety-free customer is the hallmark of an organization committed to killer customer care. Knowing what to expect and how your company works is an important step in creating that result.

Four: Look Your Customer in the Eye

The principle at work here is very much like the one discussed above in the section about smiling. Getting your employees to look your customers in the eye is even more difficult than getting them to smile. Most people are not comfortable with direct eye contact. It makes them feel as though they're being too aggressive and intrusive. Of course, that's not how customers see it at all.

The payoff for getting your employees to engage in this "unnatural" behavior is that your customers will feel more important. They'll feel as though attention is being given to them. If eye contact is not made consistently, you run the risk of having customers perceive your employees as rude, untrustworthy, or disinterested.

The Mark Two Dinner Theater in Orlando is a terrific example of a business that lets the customer know what to expect. Upon your arrival at the theater, the ticket taker asks if you've ever attended one of Mark Two's productions. If you haven't, you're given a step-by-step explanation of what you can expect. You're told about seating, ordering your meal, intermission, and even what your coffee and dessert options are. As a result, every first-time customer is immediately comfortable, relaxed, and ready to enjoy a pleasant show and a great meal.

Like teaching your employees to smile, this is primarily a matter of explicitly stating your expectations, then monitoring how well they're being met. A very effective strategy in getting the results you want in both areas is to randomly catch employees doing it right and then praising and rewarding them lavishly. (You'll find much more about this strategy in Chapter 23.)

Five: Follow the Customer's Lead

At its most basic level, killer customer care is whatever your customer decides it is. You can create systems and procedures that are effective for most customers, most of the time. (After all, that's why you're reading this book.) When it comes down to that ultimate level of granularity, though—the one-on-one, face-to-face interaction between one of your employees and one of your customers—the most carefully planned systems and procedures often need to be subordinated to that single customer's preferences.

Most customers will want to be engaged and paid attention to by your employees most of the time. However, some will prefer to be left alone. Killer customer care is definitely not a one-size-fits-all undertaking. Make sure your employees allow your customers to set the tone for any interaction. What might seem like attentiveness to your employee might make one of these "Greta Garbo" customers feel as though they're being stalked. An important key to success is to be attentive to that customer's preferences and sensitive to his or her boundaries. Your business's general policies and procedures about interacting with customers should not take precedence over respecting your customer's preferences and staying well within the boundaries of his or her comfort zone.

Six: Be Available

Even if customers seem to want to explore what your business has to offer by themselves and at their own pace (but *especially* if they don't), there will usually come a time when they have a question or want some assistance. When that time comes, they shouldn't have to file a missing persons report with the local police department. Ideally, your employees should be within earshot of your customer. If that's not always possible, someone should at least be visible.

Nothing puts a damper on a customer's perception of killer customer care faster than that customer having to wander around searching for someone to answer a question or check a price. Ironically (and, let's face it, maddeningly), this is especially true for those customers who, just moments before, were emphatic about wanting to be left alone.

Seven: Live Customer Trumps the Telephone

There is a Pavlovian quality to the way most people react to the telephone. The television show *Candid Camera* has gotten a great deal of mileage over the years out of scenarios in which passersby cannot resist answering a ringing pay phone on the street, even when the chances of the call being for them is approximately—zero!

Of course, there are compelling business reasons to be responsive to the needs of customers who use the phone to contact your business (and we'll discuss the principles for handling the telephone effectively in Chapter 11.). But a small amount of reflection is all it ought to take for you to evaluate the relative importance of a customer who visits your business in person and one who calls on the phone. In general, you know little about a customer on the other end of a phone call. They may or may not be qualified to purchase your products and services. In fact, they may or may not be seriously interested in what you have to offer. They have invested no real time or energy in contacting you. This doesn't mean they're not serious or they're not interested. It just means you and your employees have limited data on which to make a determination.

The people visiting your business in person, on the other hand, have probably invested some amount of time and effort in getting there. As they walk in the door, you might not necessarily know all that much about them, but you know that they're real and that they've made some sort of effort to get there. Working with a limited amount of data, it is still clear that the customer who's there in person is probably a better prospect than the one on the phone. At the very least, you owe that "live" person the consideration of your attention while he or she is there.

Direct Costs

Remarkably, it is a common practice to ignore the customer who is in a business in person in favor of someone who calls on the phone. This just doesn't make sense. Of course, common sense should always prevail, and special circumstances might merit special treatment. In most situations, though, your employees should understand that the customer who is there in person takes precedence over the one who calls on the phone.

What do you do, then, about the customer on the phone? Use a variation of this standard explanation: "I'm with a customer right now and I'd like to give you my undivided attention. Is there a number where I can give you a call back sometime within the next ten minutes?" The overwhelming majority of customers with serious inquiries will find this response perfectly acceptable. And the response has two big advantages for your business. First, it allows your employee to be attentive to both customers. (The alternative invariably leaves both customers feeling they did not receive the attention they wanted or deserved.) A second ancillary advantage to this response is that it weeds out frivolous phone inquiries, allowing your employees to spend more of their time with serious, qualified customers.

Eight: Stay Focused on the Customer

When a customer visits your business, the principles of killer customer care dictate that he or she ought to receive the undivided attention of your employees. Your employee training and orientation should make it clear that casual, social conversations between employees are not appropriate when customers are present.

It might come as a shock to some employees, but a customer getting a haircut has little or no interest in what happened at the nightclub last night. While the customer might ostensibly be there for a haircut, she's also expecting to be the center of the haircutter's attention for as long as she is sitting there in the chair.

Nine: Capture Customer Information for Follow-up Contact

In the next chapter, we're going to explore strategies and techniques for systematizing your customer care efforts. All of those strategies and techniques are predicated on your having adequate and appropriate information about your customers with which to work. Therefore, capturing information about your customers that can be used later needs to be a regular and important part of every face-to-face customer contact.

It's silly, when you think about it, to go through all the trouble and expense of convincing a customer to visit your business, then allowing that customer to leave without a way to contact him or her again!

The basic strategy for doing this successfully involves identifying something of value that you can offer your customer in exchange for their information. Many supermarkets, for example, offer a discount card. Some businesses offer to send the customer a newsletter or some other infor-

*T*he information you'll want to collect from your customers includes (but is not limited to):

- Name
- Address
- Phone number
- E-mail address
- Products or services that interest the customer

mation. Whatever "hook" you decide on, make sure it's something that represents real value to your customer.

Ten: Prepare for All of the Most Likely Scenarios

When you consider the number of scenarios that might possibly occur during a typical week's worth of face-to-face customer interaction, it is virtually infinite. When it comes to customers (especially in a retail environment), anything can happen—and usually does over a long enough period of time! On the other hand, if you stop to think about it, the vast majority of your customer interactions probably can be summarized into a very finite few general situations. Usually, a customer wants to:

- Buy something immediately
- Buy something at some point in the future
- Get pricing or other information
- Solve a particular problem
- Register a complaint

You can probably add a few scenarios of your own to this list. The point, though, is that most of the time, your employees will be dealing repeatedly with a limited number of scenarios. Your face-to-face contacts are much more likely to produce a result of killer customer care if your employees are thoroughly prepared for these frequently occurring situations. Your objective is not to lock your employees into a rigid set of behaviors but to get them practiced and prepared for the scenarios they're most likely to encounter.

Practice these situations over and over again during your regular meetings or training sessions. This practice is the equivalent of a shortstop practicing his fielding of ground balls. In each case, the objective is to create responses that are effective and instinctive.

Looking Ahead

It is practice that will allow your individual employees to consistently respond to customers effectively. But if you want your business, as an *organization*, to achieve the same result, you'll need to implement systems that will allow it to do so. That is the subject we'll be covering in Chapter 8.

WHY YOU NEED TO SYSTEMATIZE YOUR APPROACH TO CUSTOMER CARE

CREATING A PROCESS FOR DELIVERING CUSTOMER CARE

Before we examine the rationale for systematizing your customer care mechanisms and discuss some simple, highly effective strategies for doing so, let's do a short, instructive exercise. Put on your marketing hat for just a moment to evaluate a few ideas for a hypothetical advertising campaign. The parameters for the campaign are simple. It's going to tout the customer service performance of an imaginary company, but it must be completely honest and straightforward in doing so. Here are the results of some initial brainstorming:

- We'll come through for you almost all the time.
- Our company meets its customers' objectives very often.
- We're no worse than anyone else in our industry.
- Our customer service is extremely adequate.
- We only allow a few things to fall through the cracks.

Well? Does anything there sound appealing to you? Do you think any of these slogans has the potential to energize or motivate a group of potential customers?

Of course not. But it won't take too much reflection for you to realize that the real problem in this hypothetical situation is not the construction of the marketing message. The real problem is the underlying reality of the performance that this make-believe company is attempting to promote. The stark reality we must all confront is that in today's hypercompetitive marketplace, "good enough" is simply no longer good enough.

Levels of customer care performance that once seemed lofty are no longer sufficient. Yesterday's superior customer care standards are barely adequate by today's standards. If your company is to achieve levels of performance that can fairly be described by the phrase killer customer care, then you'll need to reach a standard of performance that is, for all practical purposes, flawless.

But even the best of intentions are not enough to get you there. To reach the level of care that we consider killer customer care, you'll need to supplement the performance of your employees with systematized processes that leave nothing to chance and that allow nothing to fall through the cracks. For the sake of convenience, we'll refer to these processes as "systems." In this context, however, we are not necessarily talking about computer systems, even though computers are certainly the most common and usually the most efficient and cost-effective way to implement a systematized process.

In this chapter, we're going to discuss the principle of systematizing processes. We'll also take a look at some guidelines for designing systems to accumulate customer information and handle incidents of customer contact.

> Is 99.99 percent good enough? Well, a 99.99 percent level of performance would allow for one or two crashes a day at O'Hare Airport in Chicago. Granted, the implications of a lapse in your company's customer care performance may not be as devastating, but what is the virtue in settling for a standard that is less than the best you can achieve? And that's especially true when better customer care performance costs no more than mediocre performance.

Another important system is the one you use to handle customer problems and complaints. The principles of systemization apply there, too, but an effective customer complaint system is so important that it will be addressed separately in Chapter 20.

What's So Special about a System?

Let's begin with a brief definition:

A systematized process—or system—is a self-contained set of interrelated steps that work together in a predetermined manner to achieve a specific result.

Each aspect of this definition is important. *Self-contained* means your system functions like an airtight enclosure. Once something is in the system, it cannot get out unless and until it is supposed to. In other words, nothing falls through the cracks.

Interrelated steps that work together means that systems, by definition, are multistep procedures, usually ones in which one step depends on or flows from the previous step.

Predetermined manner means you know in advance how you want these steps to work. When Event "A" occurs, no one needs to wonder about how it will get handled. The system is designed to anticipate all of the most likely possibilities and provide for them.

Achieve a specific result means the "output" of the system is something that is designed to be of value to your customer, to your business, or to both.

Definitions like this are academic and abstract. Let's take a look at how these concepts can be applied to a couple of specific systems that a business uses every day.

Getting Personal with Your Customers

In the last chapter, we touched on the need for capturing information about every customer who visits your business. After all, getting a customer to visit your business in the first place is time consuming and expensive. It makes no sense to succeed with the most difficult part of your marketing only to allow that customer to walk out the door anonymously. After all, killer customer care is difficult to achieve if you don't have a way to get in touch with your customers. This principle applies to every single contact a customer makes with your business, whether it's in person, on the phone, or over the Internet. Let's see what it means to systematize the process of accumulating customer information.

Defining the Result

The best place to start in designing any system is by defining the end result you want to achieve. What is the specific result you'd want to achieve in this instance?

Here, you want to create a database of information about active and potential customers that you can use to address the needs of those customers more effectively (something of value to your customers) and to market to those customers more efficiently (something of value to your business). Your particular interpretation of those objectives will dictate the precise information you will ideally want to accumulate. In general, though, there are several pieces of information that it's always useful to have:

- Name
- Address
- Phone number
- E-mail address
- Is the contact an active customer or a prospect?
- How did the customer hear about you?

- What product/service did the customer ask about?
- Any other information it would be useful for you to track

But whatever information you decide you want, the creation of the database is the specific result you want to accomplish.

Determining the Steps

Next, you'll want to determine the steps you'll need to take in order to create the result you want. In this scenario, you can begin by identifying all of the different ways a customer or potential customer might come into contact with your business. These can include:

- In person
- E-mail
- Web site response
- Telephone
- Mail

Identifying Best Methods

Once you've compiled a list of how you and potential customers can connect, your next step is to identify the best way(s) to accumulate the information you need for each method of contact. Figure 8-1 shows what the result of this exercise might look like for a retail store.

The procedures in this hypothetical example are somewhat less detailed than the ones you'll create for your own real world business, but they illustrate how the principles of system design work. The important thing is to put a procedure in place that everyone in your company understands and executes each and every time a new customer comes into contact with your business.

In Person	Every customer is entered into the company's database at the cash register. Sales personnel are instructed to offer other store visitors (i.e., non-buyers) a coupon for a ten percent discount on an upcoming purchase if they answer a few questions.
E-mail	E-mail from new customers is answered (if necessary) and forwarded to a centralized administrative assistant. The sender's name and e-mail address are checked against the existing database by the administrative assistant and entered if they are not already there. The new contact is then offered a discount coupon via e-mail for completing a brief questionnaire.
Web Site Response	E-mails from new customers are answered (if necessary) and forwarded to a centralized administrative assistant. Senders' names and e-mail addresses are checked against an existing database by the administrative assistant and entered if they are not already there. The new contact is then offered a discount coupon via e-mail for completing a brief questionnaire.
Telephone	Call center personnel are trained to accumulate database information during the course of handling a routine call.
Mail	Name and address are entered into the database by the administrative assistant. A coupon offer and questionnaire requesting more complete information are returned via mail.

FIGURE 8-1. Best ways to accumulate information for each contact

Coordinating Customer Connections

Another facet of your business that can benefit from systematization is communicating with your customers. If there's one aspect of your business where you don't want anything to fall through the cracks, it's customer communication. Your ability to handle customer communication flawlessly will underscore your commitment to killer cus-

> *Most in-person communications can and should be handled in "real time," according to the principles outlined in the last chapter. In those instances, of course, there is no series of "interrelated steps" to follow, so the concept of systematization isn't relevant. The desirability of installing a system comes into play when your customer makes contact through e-mail or by the telephone.*

tomer care more effectively than almost anything else you can do. In particular, this discussion refers to the handling of those communications that are initiated by the customer with the expectation of some type of response from your company.

Let's follow the same general procedure we used a moment ago. What are your objectives when a customer contacts your business? In other words, what should your end result look like? Here are a few elements that would probably be part of most business's objectives:

- Identify the customer
- Define the nature of the contact
- Refer the information to the appropriate person for response or resolution
- Verify the result of the contact

Now that we understand where we want to go, let's give some thought to how we might get there.

The most striking feature about our first objective, to *identify the customer*, is that it's the process we discussed just a moment ago. As you begin to systematize various elements of your customer care program, you'll find this duplication is not uncommon. In fact, you should fully expect to find related, overlapping processes and should take advantage of that opportunity when you do. In many ways, you can think of your various systems as being modular. When the opportunity presents itself, as it does here, you can easily take an existing system and plug it in somewhere else.

When it is time to *define the nature of the contact*, the most effective approach is also a variation of a concept that we've already examined. If you take a moment to categorize all of the phone calls and e-mails that your business receives, the overwhelming majority of them will fall into just a few categories. Is this customer calling with a complaint? (If so, as I mentioned earlier, we'll devote an entire chapter to that special category of customer contact in Chapter 20). Is this contact a request for product information? For pricing information? Is there a service or repair issue involved? Whether you've ever analyzed it or not, your business has its own special, finite list of reasons that customers call or write. Once you've identified the elements your list contains, you can create an appropriate procedure for each item on the list.

Moving through our list of objectives, the next thing your employee will want to do in this scenario is to *refer the information (or the caller) to the appropriate person for response or resolution*. If the person who fields the phone call or e-mail can resolve the issue or provide the information, that's a much more straightforward and reliable procedure than handing the issue off to another employee or department. Therefore, you'll want to provide that front-line person with as much information and as many tools as possible to get the job done.

Verifying the Result

Your final step in the process of handling customer contacts is to *verify the result of the contact*. It is this step that ensures a level of service that meets the standard of killer customer care. Simply put, this step involves establishing a feedback mechanism that provides you with positive confirmation that every customer's contact has been handled properly.

If a customer calls in with a service request, that request might get logged into an "Open Items" file and stay there until word comes back from the service department that everything's been handled. This file allows you or someone on your management team to regularly review the status of

Refer the Issue, Not the Caller

Sometimes, a handoff is unavoidable. When that's the case, a fundamental principle of killer customer care is to refer the issue, not the caller, whenever possible.

Consider a hypothetical situation from the customer's perspective. (And, as you do so, think also of your own experiences as a customer and consumer.) In this instance, let's imagine a conversation that takes place between the local office of an insurance company and a customer who would like to make a change in her automobile insurance coverage:

"It's a great day at Acme Insurance. This is Jane Hathaway. How may we help you today?"

"This is Mrs. Clampett. My son, Jethro, just turned 16 years old. I'd like to add him to our insurance policy as an additional driver."

"Do you have a policy with our office, Mrs. Clampett?"

"Yes. My husband and I have both of our cars insured with you."

"And what is your address?"

"We're at 518 Crestview Drive."

"Okay. I just want to make sure we have the right records here. Your husband's name is Jedd?"

"Yes, that's right."

"And Jethro will be an additional driver on both cars?"

"Yes. You should have his information there.

I contacted you when he got his learner's permit."

"Yes, Mrs. Clampett, I have it all right here..."

Up until now, Acme insurance is doing just fine. Jane Hathaway has identified the customer and verified that she is in the customer database maintained at the office. She has also ascertained exactly what her customer is calling about. It is at this point, however, that things begin to go wrong.

"Mrs. Clampett, if you'll hold on for just a moment, I'll transfer you over to Mr. Drysdale. He can help you out."

"But all I need ..."

It's too late. Ms. Hathaway has already put Mrs. Clampett on hold. The wait isn't too onerous, though, and a few minutes later, Mr. Drysdale, the general agent, gets on the line.

"This is Milburn Drysdale. How can I help you?"

"I was telling Miss Hathaway that I'd like to have my son added to our insurance coverage."

"I'd be happy to take care of that for you. With whom am I speaking ...?"

Do you see the problem? Before this conversation is over, Mrs. Clampett will have repeated for Mr. Drysdale everything she had already said to Miss Hathaway.

Rather than referring the customer to the

office's general agent, Miss Hathaway could have simply recorded the information she had collected, along with any other relevant information that might have been required, and allowed her customer to get off the phone. She could then have given it all to the general agent who would have been able to process the customer's request. When you refer the issue, not the caller, the customer is not bounced around, transferred, or made to repeat her story.

pending customer issues and to monitor the timeliness with which incoming customer issues are addressed.

The Art of Systematization

As you can probably gather from reviewing these examples, establishing structured systems as a part of your company's approach to customer care is as much art as it is science. The bad news is there are no cookie cutters to follow. You'll need to assess your company's specific requirements and design unique systems based on what you find. The good news is that doing so will give your company a real competitive advantage based on your ability to consistently provide that flawless level of service we call killer customer care.

Looking Ahead

So far, we have laid an important foundation by examining the principles of killer customer care from a relatively high level. Now, we're ready to drill down to the next level of detail. In the next chapter, we will begin by examining some proven techniques you can use to train your frontline employees to consistently deliver on your company's vision and promise of killer customer care.

SECTION III

▲ ▲ ▲

IMPLEMENTING YOUR KILLER CUSTOMER CARE PROGRAM

TRAINING THE TROOPS ON THE FRONT LINE

CREATING A CUSTOMER CARE CULTURE ◀

*L*et's start off with a simple premise, one we've mentioned briefly before: Most employees want to do a good job most of the time, particularly when it comes to interacting with customers. When well-intentioned employees are consistently failing to deliver exceptional results in this critical area, the cause can almost always be traced to one of two culprits.

The first suspect would be that the company's culture and systems are not structured to foster an environment of customer care, and the fundamental steps for dealing with that situation were outlined in Chapter 2.

The second reason employees often don't offer killer customer care is because they have not been trained adequately. In this chapter and the next, we'll explore some strategies and techniques you can use to make sure your employees know how to translate your vision of killer customer care into productive and gratifying interactions with your customers. This chapter will examine training principles for getting killer customer care performance from your "front-line" employees, those whose jobs explicitly entail daily interactions with customers. Salespeople, cashiers, and receptionists are some examples of front-line employees. In Chapter 10, we'll take a look at training strategies for your other employees, the folks who are not on the front line but come into contact with your customers from time to time.

> *If you don't believe that most employees generally want to deliver good custumor care, then you may have a problem in the area of recruiting and hiring. That's an important topic, but one that is somewhat outside the scope of this book, so you might want to consider doing some research in that area.*

If we accept the premise stated above, that most employees want to do a good job, then what problem with employee training results in a level of customer care that is nothing short of abysmal at many businesses?

The answer is fairly straightforward. The biggest problem with most employees' customer care training is—to put it succinctly—*there isn't any!*

The Disconnect on the Front Line

Although it's difficult to find a company that doesn't at least pay lip service to customer care, most companies spend much more time teaching new employees how to operate the cash register than how to take care of customers. The most charitable description of this situation could be benign neglect. These businesses assume new employees will somehow innately understand the general principles of customer care. Even if that were somehow true—which, through no fault of the employee, usually isn't—these companies then engage in genuinely fanciful thinking when they further assume their new employees will know how to translate general customer care principles into specific behaviors that are appropriate in their particular industry and in their particular place of business.

Basing a business's customer care performance on this unlikely set of assumptions usually produces the result we described a moment ago: Abysmal. If your business is going to deliver killer customer care, then *you'll* need to do better. You'll need a training plan that gives your employees the foundational understanding and the tools to create the result you desire.

An effective approach to training front-line employees will reflect the needs of your particular business. In addition to a curriculum that covers the mechanics of each employee's responsibilities, you'll want to make sure each front-line employee's training includes ample time for you to:

- Reemphasize the importance of killer customer care
- Provide general guidelines for interactions with customers
- Identify the scenarios employees will most likely encounter
- Detail the specific behaviors and outcomes you expect in each scenario
- Engage in role-playing and simulations
- Allow your employees to use their own good judgment to make decisions
- Tell lots and lots of stories

Reemphasize the Importance of Killer Customer Care

An employee's initial training and orientation is precisely where you'll want to implement the principles we examined in Chapter 2. because it's the most effective time to set the tone for what you expect during his or her entire tenure with your company. That initial training is precisely the right time to firmly establish in your employee's mind the degree to which your business is committed to providing killer customer care. But your job of instilling a killer customer care culture will be significantly easier if your employee understands *why* your business is committed to customer care and the benefits that accrue to the company and its employees when customer care pervades the work environment.

Don't make the mistake of assuming that employees will accept and internalize your priorities just because they get paychecks from you. If you want to establish a culture of killer customer care, you must evangelize that culture constantly. If you want your employees to genuinely buy in to your message, you'll need to demonstrate the benefits they'll gain by doing so. Hint: not getting fired is not a benefit. It is a thinly veiled threat.

Expounding on the benefits customer care creates for the company is a natural message for most managers. Itemizing the benefits customer care creates for employees is usually a bit more difficult. What are the benefits of killer customer care for your employees? They include a more positive work environment, a more stable company, more employee opportunities, and greater income opportunities, to name just a few. You can certainly compile your own list. The important thing is to show your employees why customer care is not just good for the company, but also good for them.

Provide General Guidelines for Interactions with Customers

The best to way to structure your training is to move from broad concepts to specific techniques and examples. This method allows your employees to gain familiarity with general concepts and then see how those concepts might be applied in specific situations.

The general concepts in this instance are your principles for customer care. What qualities do you most want your business and your employees to project? What standards do you want them to use when they're confronted with an unfamiliar or unanticipated situation?

Although there will be many variables in the details of your business's approach to killer customer care, the important thing is to clearly outline the general guidelines you want your employees to consider in their day-to-day interactions with your customers.

Get the Training Right

Although the principles at this stage of your training are supposed to be general, it's possible to be too general. And even a seemingly self-evident principle might require careful consideration and a bit of clarification. For example, you could discuss the need for employees to be polite when speaking with customers. At first glance, that principle might seem to be self-evident. But if you dig just a bit more deeply, you'll uncover a few underlying issues worth addressing.

Does politeness dictate that an employee should address a customer by name? If you believe that it does, is using the customer's first name appropriate or should the employee adopt a more formal approach? Does the customer's age or gender make a difference?

Of course, there aren't any universal answers to questions like those. The right answers for your business will depend on the market you serve and the image you're trying to convey. A coffeehouse in a college town will answer those questions differently than an expensive French restaurant in an upscale neighborhood of a large city.

Identify the Scenarios Employees Will Most Likely Encounter

We've discussed this principle already, so there's no need to spend a great deal of time on it here. The basic idea is that, in every business, the vast majority of interactions with employees will fall into a very finite number of categories. As you prepare the training curriculum for your front-line employees, you'll need to compile a list of the specific situations that account for most of the interactions your employees are likely to have with your customers. Unless your business is unusual in some fundamental way, this list will be relatively short and will account for a large percentage of your business's customer interactions, far more than the familiar eighty/twenty ratio you might expect.

This list will provide the foundation for the next element of your front-line employees' training program that we'll discuss.

Detail the Specific Behaviors and Outcomes You Expect in Each Scenario

Once you've compiled your business's unique list of "most likely" scenarios, you are now in a position to take your front-line employee training to a level of greater specificity. Let your employees know this next phase of their training is going to prepare them for most of the customer interactions they'll encounter. This message and approach will enhance their confidence in much the same way that the confidence of a boxer is enhanced by training with a sparring partner who lets him prepare for his upcoming opponent's likely tactics and style.

At this point in your training program, you'll be able to teach your employee how to handle each of the specific scenarios he or she will likely face. Let's say you're training a retail employee on what to do when a customer brings a product back to the store, a situation that will no doubt be on your short list of likely scenarios. What information should the employee elicit from the customer? What documentation would you like to have? What happens if the customer doesn't have the necessary receipts? What if the customer wants an exchange? What about a refund? What if the merchandise has been used? These are all issues you'll want to address in your training.

Unexpected Benefits from Your Training Plan

It is worth mentioning here that the very exercise of developing this training curriculum may yield unexpected benefits, particularly when senior management gets actively involved.

While undertaking this process, one consumer electronics store chain began to wrestle with the sometimes sticky issue of how to handle customers who lost their receipts. When senior managers got involved, they decided to bypass the issue altogether by maintaining their purchase records electronically. As a result, the chain's killer customer care quotient was raised dramatically.

Engage in Role-Playing and Simulations

The purpose of defining most likely scenarios is not to create a policies and procedures manual. In fact, such a manual is seldom a good omen when it comes to customer care. Employees and managers at companies that compile them often become fixated on following the rules rather than creating positive outcomes.

A better approach is to give your employees ample practice in applying the guidelines you've provided. There is no better way to provide that practice than to engage in role-playing and situational simulations. This training technique is versatile, engaging, and extremely effective. It is applicable to the widest possible range of situations. Even more important is the fact that it produces employees who are prepared to deliver killer customer care even when the customer deviates from the script.

Role-playing is most effective when it's done in small groups—no more than four or five employees—and moderated by a manager or senior employee experienced with a wide variety of customer care situations.

One trainee at a time is selected to play the role of an employee in a specific customer care situation that has been discussed in previous training sessions. For example, the trainee might be told he or she is assisting a customer who wants to open a new account. The moderator plays the role of the customer. The moderator's agenda may be a straightforward reflection of the role-playing scenario given to the trainee or it may reflect a hidden agenda that the trainee can uncover with appropriate interaction.

At the end of the role-playing exercise, the trainee is evaluated by the other trainees in the group and, finally, by the moderator.

Sales organizations have long used role-playing as an

effective training tool. Your customer care training for front-line employees will benefit immeasurably from your use of this same proven training technique.

Allow Your Employees to Use Their Own Good Judgment to Make Decisions

Throughout your training, it is important to communicate to your employees that there is no script they are required to follow. They should approach every customer interaction with an appreciation for your company's values, an understanding of the guidelines you've provided, and the confidence to use their own good judgment in providing customer care.

An atmosphere of killer customer care cannot be achieved when employees are overly worried about the consequences of an incorrect decision. If your employees are afraid to make decisions, they simply won't make them, and your customer care standards will suffer.

Front-line employees become effective when they understand that they are empowered to make decisions on behalf of your business and in the interest of its customers. Your training will prepare them to make those decisions and should communicate to them that they are encouraged to do so.

Tell Lots and Lots of Stories

Few techniques engage the interest of your employees and communicate your business's values to them than stories about how other employees and managers have delivered on the promise of killer customer care. An important part of your training repertoire should be a seemingly endless trove of stories about customer care heroes

The best stories are about your employees, but don't be

reluctant to tell stories about other companies (even competitors) as well. Stories communicate values in powerful, almost visceral ways. When they are selected carefully, they are remembered and repeated frequently. Over time, they become part of your company's folklore. Every company that has achieved legendary levels of customer care has used this powerful tool as part of its training program.

One Final Word about Customer Care Training

It is a process, not an event. Certainly, your new employees will receive a concentrated dose of customer care training when they come on board. That's not only necessary but also appropriate. You'll want to give your new employee a solid foundation in customer care right from the start. But when the initial training is completed, your mission is by no means finished.

Customer care training needs to be an ongoing part of your employee's work experience. Like bathing or brushing teeth, it's simply something that ought to be done regularly. After all, you can't be too clean, you can't have teeth that are too white, and you can't be too good at killer customer care.

Looking Ahead

Now that we've reviewed the principles of effectively providing customer care training for your front-line employees, let's turn our attention to your other employees. In Chapter 10, we'll look at techniques for providing customer care training for everyone else in your organization.

TRAINING EVERYONE ELSE ON THE PRINCIPLES OF CUSTOMER CARE

EVERYONE SUPPORTS THE CUSTOMERS IN ONE WAY OR ANOTHER

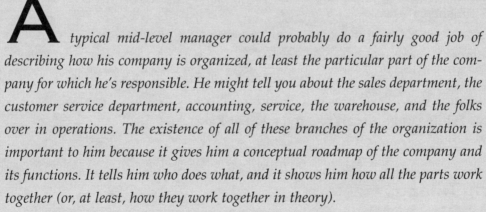

A typical mid-level manager could probably do a fairly good job of describing how his company is organized, at least the particular part of the company for which he's responsible. He might tell you about the sales department, the customer service department, accounting, service, the warehouse, and the folks over in operations. The existence of all of these branches of the organization is important to him because it gives him a conceptual roadmap of the company and its functions. It tells him who does what, and it shows him how all the parts work together (or, at least, how they work together in theory).

This typical mid-level manager relies on this roadmap as a management tool. Its pigeonholes and relationships seem important to him because they've been handed down from upper management and provide him with foundation for understanding how things ought to work. However, the company's organizational structure often obscures another even more important fact.

Your customer doesn't care about any of that.

"It Is Your Department"

From your customer's point of view, organizational distinctions are not only meaningless, they are often annoying. When a customer has a question, an issue, or a problem, the very last thing that she wants to hear is "That's not my department."

Your customer is not interested in the ways in which your company has assigned roles and responsibilities. Instead, she sees a single company that is there, ostensibly, to help her achieve some necessary objective or desired result.

From her vantage point, if organizational roles and responsibilities exist, they should be there to serve her interest, not force her to accommodate to the organizational structure of the company.

A Guiding Principle

If the standards for killer customer care are set by our customers, then, let's acknowledge an important premise at the outset of this chapter: *everyone in your organization is responsible for customer care, regardless of whatever other specific functions they perform.* It doesn't matter where in the company a particular individual works; everyone's ultimate responsibility is to help provide superior care and service for the company's customers.

This premise follows naturally from the foundational concepts we discussed in Chapter 2. And, in the abstract, very few managers would disagree with it. As a practical matter, however, most companies tend to categorize the individuals in their work force according to whether or not they are "front-line" employees (as described in the last chapter). Employees on the front line are far more likely to receive at least some training in techniques for interacting with customers effectively.

Individuals who are not considered "front-line" employees seldom receive any training at all in effective customer interaction. There seems to be an underlying assumption that these employees don't need customer care training because they interact with customers less regularly or less frequently. However, any manager committed to providing killer customer care should recognize that this assumption is seriously flawed.

For one thing, it's certainly not a sentiment shared by your customers. If a customer has an unsatisfactory experience with one of your employees, he doesn't make a distinction between employees who are front-line and those who are not. He just wants results. And he holds all of your employees accountable for providing a high level of customer care, regardless of what their specific job titles are.

Just because an employee's contact with customers is not frequent or regular, it doesn't mean his or her customer interaction skills are not important. Often, a customer perceives interactions with an employee who is not on the front line to be more substantive than interactions with sales and customer service personnel. As a result, those

Different Employees, Different Skills

Another reason "back-room" employees need customer care training is because whatever innate customer care skills they bring to the workplace are probably less well developed than those of your front-line employees. This statement is not intended to slight individuals who don't work in jobs that put them in regular, direct contact with customers. It's merely a recognition of the fact that their aptitude for "back-room" work can often (but not always) indicate they're not comfortable with the person-to-person interaction common on the front line.

Acknowledging this difference does not imply a value judgment of your back-room employees. Your business requires people with different skills and aptitudes. But employees are not equally gifted in all areas of endeavor. If you're still skeptical, try taking your best salesperson—the one with people skills galore—and let her or him try working in the accounting department for a week.

It's not hard to see, then, that your employees who don't work with customers every day might need customer care training even more than the ones who do.

interactions can disproportionately impact the customer's perception of your company.

Killer Customer Care Is for Everyone

It is clear that *everyone* in your company needs a thorough grounding in the principles of killer customer care. And, for the most part, the training curriculum you use for your back-room employees will not be very different from the training program we examined in the last chapter. But it should address the varied backgrounds these employees bring to the workplace and the different circumstances in which they work. In addition, certain other tactics, listed below, usually need to be used.

- Evangelize killer customer care even more strongly.
- Assist employees in seeing things from the customer's perspective.
- Help employees set aside their egos.
- Pay special attention to "problem customer" situations.
- Identify as many likely encounters as possible.

Evangelize Killer Customer Care Even More Strongly

If an employee is not in contact with customers every day, it is all too easy to lose sight of the importance of customer care. An employee with a job that does not include regular contact with customers can quickly shift focus to the product or task at hand rather than on the impact the product or task has on a customer. That this danger exists with your employees who aren't on the front line is natural and doesn't suggest some sort of shortcoming on their part. It does underscore the special emphasis on customer care that needs to be a pervasive element of their training curriculum.

Make certain the training demonstrates the impact that customer care can have on the company's profitability, growth, and position in the marketplace. In addition, make sure you put a special emphasis on the impact customer care can have on your employees' own incomes and career prospects.

Your evangelization efforts for these employees should be as factual and quantified as possible because these employees will often think in a more linear fashion than will your front-line workers (a characteristic that's sometimes referred to as "left-brained"). Use graphs and charts whenever you can to illustrate the points you want to make.

Assist Employees in Seeing Things from the Customer's Perspective

When an employee isn't working with customers regularly, he can develop a perspective that is internalized. He looks at the company's policies and procedures and sees very clearly how adherence to those rules will make everyone's life easier. What sense does it make, he might wonder, to make exceptions or circumvent the established order of things?

A world filled with customers, on the other hand, is an untidy place. It is not orderly, it doesn't function on a set schedule, and it often doesn't make sense.

Your employee needs your help to see the world from the customer's point of view. The customer confers value on the intangible qualities of a transaction as well as its tangible results.

A New England retailer with a background in accounting used to argue with his customers before granting them a refund. At the end of the transaction, he assumed that they'd be satisfied with the result because they ultimately received the refund they sought. He needed help in understanding how the contentious transaction felt to his customers.

Help Employees Set Aside Their Egos

One of the most difficult aspects of customer interaction for non-front-line employees is the need to set aside one's ego in potentially contentious situations. Sometimes, it is difficult for your employees to relinquish the inclination to prove they're right, especially when it is clear to them that the customer is wrong.

Your training program needs to help your employees adopt a different, "unnatural" approach in situations that have the potential to become touchy. They need to ingrain the habit of looking at customer interactions not from the standpoint of who is right or wrong. Instead, they need to be taught how to focus on reaching the best outcome for the company, which, in turn, usually means willingly and cheerfully finding a solution that is satisfactory for the customer.

Pay Special Attention to "Problem Customer" Situations

Conventional wisdom once held that the customer is always right. That's a difficult position to take when customers are demanding or apparently unreasonable. But even though the customer may not always be right, *the customer is always the customer*. That being the case, killer customer care requires your employees to be prepared to respond to situations that might be challenging or even exasperating.

What happens when a customer is angry? What about the customer who is pushy? Or what about the customer who is apparently untruthful? Your employees who deal

As you role-play tricky customer situations in your training, it is often helpful to get your employees to consider extending the role-playing paradigm into the actual customer interaction. In other words, if ego seems to get in the way, get them to step outside of themselves when dealing with customers and adopt the role of a customer care specialist. If they can see their actions in a difficult situation in terms of a role they're playing, it's easier to get beyond the need to be "right" and to focus on getting the situation resolved.

Your training challenge is to help your employees to find some effective strategies for taking their egos out of the equation. They need to understand that, as in the timeless words of Michael Corleone, "it's business, not personal."

with customers every day are less likely to be rattled by these sorts of behaviors than those who only deal with customers occasionally. Your employees who don't function on the front lines every day need to understand that there is a wide range of undesirable customer behaviors that they will likely experience over time. It's part of the territory and shouldn't be unduly upsetting. Rather than sidestepping this issue, your training should readily acknowledge that these situations arise and prepare your employees to deal with them.

Your training should also address the issue of when it's time to escalate the matter and get someone else involved. Your employee should understand that there is no virtue in allowing a contentious situation to continue indefinitely or to spiral out of control unnecessarily. Sometimes, a tactical retreat and the summoning of reinforcements is exactly what a difficult situation requires.

Identify as Many Likely Encounters as Possible

Finally, we've already seen that a highly effective strategy for designing an environment of killer customer care is to define and plan for the scenarios that are most likely to occur. This principle is just as effective for non-front-line employees as it is for their counterparts. But while the strategy is the same, the scenarios will probably be entirely different.

Under what circumstances is one of your customers likely to come into contact with someone from accounting or from the warehouse or from operations? Identify those situations. Then, role-play with your employees about how they can best be handled.

Looking Ahead

Now that you're familiar with the concepts of developing effective training strategies to teach your employees killer customer care, it's time to turn our attention to a special tool that is ubiquitous in business. It is one that's critically important to almost every business and can be a highly effective tool for both your business and your customers. Simultaneously, however, this tool offers an almost endless series of opportunities to enrage and frustrate your customers. Of course, we're talking about the telephone, which we'll explore in Chapter 11.

LEARN HOW TO ANSWER THE TELEPHONE

DO IT RIGHT WHEN TALKING TO CUSTOMERS ON THE TELEPHONE

O ver the years, countless motivational speakers have maintained that the Chinese words for "danger" and "opportunity" combine to form the Chinese ideogram for the word "crisis." Because very few motivational speakers are fluent in Chinese (or even reasonably familiar with it), you'd be justified in suspecting that this motivational cliché is a sham. Well, against all odds and expectations, the characters for "danger" and "opportunity" do, indeed, combine to form "crisis" in Chinese.

In the context of customer care, however, the combination of "danger" and "opportunity" might produce an entirely different picture—a picture of a telephone. That's because communicating with customers on the phone promises great opportunity when handled correctly but poses great danger if it's not.

Like most tools, the telephone is neither inherently positive nor inherently negative. Its impact depends on how it's used. In this chapter, we'll examine some strategies and techniques for using the phone effectively to augment customer care. We'll also outline some common traps you'll want to avoid in order to prevent this powerful tool from wounding you.

When considering the phone and its implications for your business's ability to provide killer customer care, you should remember two important facts. First, remember that the telephone is what brings many of your customers and potential customers that critical, often determinative, first impression of your business. Second, remember that there is nothing to prevent a customer from hanging up the phone and disappearing from your business forever.

The Critical First Impression

When it comes to establishing an overall environment of killer customer care, the telephone often sets the tone for much of the business relationship that follows. Think of your own business for a moment. How often does a customer's first contact with your business come over the telephone? If your business is like most, the answer is "Fairly often."

After all, you're probably spending a lot of money and a great deal of energy to create that specific result. Retail businesses often devote a large chunk of their advertising and marketing budgets to ads in the Yellow Pages or other phone directories. Even when businesses advertise in other media, they will often use "telephone-centric" ads. Businesses will often devote a large percentage of airtime in their television and radio spots to repeating their phone number so customers can remember it. Newspaper ads are

> *The* telephone is a potent, user-friendly, real-time communication tool. It is ubiquitous, an ordinary and accepted part of virtually every environment that many of us take for granted because it is so familiar. In fact, it is the telephone's very ubiquity that makes it so powerful because there is no faster, easier way to connect with customers than by phone.
>
> On the other hand, when used improperly, the telephone can alienate and infuriate existing customers and ward off potential customers you've never even met.

almost always designed to feature a business's phone number prominently, displaying it in large type placed strategically in the ad so it's easy to find. Most businesses maintain one or more toll-free numbers, allowing customers to contact them at no charge from anywhere in the country.

In fact, it is nothing short of astonishing that so many businesses spend so much money on generating customer calls, then devote so little time and attention to making sure those calls are handled effectively when they arrive.

Whether you've prepared for it or not, those first few seconds on the phone create a powerful impression for your customer about what it might be like to do business with your company. Your customer is considering several things while on the phone with your company, including:

- Does this company sound attentive?
- Does this company seem competent in handling and routing the call?
- Is the person at the other end of the phone listening to what's being said?
- Do the employees sound friendly?
- Does the company care enough to have a living, breathing human being answer the phone?

Sometimes Customers Are Irrational

Here's an important principle of customer relations that's worth keeping in mind: when customers don't have much insight or information about the intrinsic quality and value of your products and services, they will make judgments about your business based on what little information they have, even if that information is not precisely relevant.

You might produce the greatest widgets in the world, but if you do a poor job of answering the phone, your customer may evaluate you on that fact alone and decide to take his business elsewhere. That's not fair or even necessarily rational, but it is a reality of customer relations you'd be wise to accommodate.

You might argue that one phone call cannot possibly convey a true picture of the quality of your business, and you might very well be right. Unfortunately, you do not get to choose the benchmarks your customer will use to evaluate you, particularly in the earliest stages of contact. That privilege belongs to your customer and your customer alone.

Easy to Disconnect

The companies that market time-share vacation properties are often extremely generous with the premiums they offer prospects in order to get them to listen to a sales presentation. All-expense-paid weekend vacation packages or television sets are common enticements. Why are they so munificent when offering a sales proposition that is usually met with stiff resistance from prospects? Because they understand that getting a prospect to listen to an entire sales presentation gives them time to tell their story completely and dramatically increases the likelihood of making the sale. And that's why the generous premiums are distributed *after* the sales presentation, not before. The premiums act like "golden handcuffs," keeping the prospect around through something he or she might otherwise be inclined to miss.

What does this have to do with the telephone? It underscores the fact that a customer's critical first contact with your business often takes place through a medium over which you have almost no control. The phone's most important characteristic is that it's extremely easy to hang up. Your only effective strategy for engaging customers on the phone so that you can ultimately lure them into a closer relationship with your business is to ensure all telephone interactions are as redolent of killer customer care as you can possibly make them.

What about Existing Customers?

Although the benefits of utilizing the phone effectively are particularly important when dealing with new customers, your ability to interact effectively on the phone will strengthen your relationships with existing customers as well. It's just as easy for existing customers as it is for new customers to hang up and call elsewhere when they are dissatisfied with the quality of a telephone interaction.

Beyond that, poor phone techniques represent a squandered opportunity to address the needs of existing customers, to make them feel special and appreciated. All it takes is the skillful use of certain new telephone technologies combined with your commitment to use the phone as a uniquely powerful tool for providing killer customer care.

Use Technology Judiciously

The remarkable technologies that power today's phone systems can do impressive things. However, if your goal is killer customer care rather than efficiency, then it's important to remember that just because something is possible doesn't mean it's desirable. Even a useful technology is not always appropriate, and an approach that's efficient is not always effective.

Auto-Attendant

Such is the case with a technology known as "automated attendant" or "auto-attendant." These systems replace or augment the "human" receptionist. They answer a company's phones and direct callers to route themselves—via touchtone keypad or speech recognition access—to specific individuals, departments, and automated process applications.

Use Technology Wisely

Customers aren't stupid. They don't believe it for a minute when the saccharin voice of the auto-attendant system says, "Your call is important to us." They know that if their call were really important, they would be talking to a real, live person, not listening to an automated attendant.

They also understand that the phrase "Please listen to this entire message as our menu options have changed" translates into "We have absolutely no intention of making this system either easy or convenient for you, and we have no regard whatsoever for your time." If you're absolutely determined to use auto-attendant (don't say you haven't been warned), then at least make sure you're not insulting the intelligence of your customer at the other end of the phone.

The following is a complete and comprehensive list of the times when the use of an auto-attendant is appropriate and consistent with the principles of killer customer care.

- After business hours when no one is available to answer the phone

That's it. If you're serious about delivering killer customer care, then your phone should be answered by a real, live person during business hours. Period.

Here is the plain, unvarnished truth: most of the time, your customers hate auto-attendants, even those that are well designed and intelligently implemented. Moreover, the overwhelming majority of auto-attendant systems are neither well designed nor intelligently implemented. In fact, if reason and common sense didn't insist otherwise, an impartial observer might conclude that most of these systems were designed to deliberately frustrate customers.

Voice Mail

Voice mail is a terrific technology when used properly. Specifically, that means voice mail is a terrific technology when used as a repository for messages for an employee who is unavailable. The challenge with voice mail is that your employee and your customer often have different ideas about what constitutes being "unavailable."

Your customer is probably naïve enough to think that "unavailable" means your employee is not in the office. In many businesses, however, "unavailable" means the employee is not in the mood to talk to a customer. This particular bit of laziness (or cowardice, depending on the circumstances) is even easier in a business that handles its incoming calls with an auto-attendant system, because there's no receptionist around to notice that calls aren't getting answered.

If your business is committed to delivering killer customer care, then your voice mail system should only be used to serve your customers more effectively, not to hide from them. If you find an employee with her "Do Not Disturb" button on, she ought to have an extremely persuasive explanation.

Caller ID

Caller ID is a relatively pedestrian technology and doesn't require a sophisticated phone system. In fact, most of your employees probably use it at home. Combined with your business's existing information systems (see Chapter 8), it can be an impressive tool for caring for your existing customers, especially if your business engages primarily in consumer sales.

When a customer calls your store, the phone number recognized by your caller ID system can be automatically compared with phone numbers in your company's customer database. If there's a match, the corresponding customer record can be automatically pulled up by the system and displayed for the employee answering the phone call. Depending on the robustness of your customer information system, that record can include information such as the customer's transaction history with your business or a list of any outstanding orders or service issues.

This simple combination of two common technologies allows your employee to be much more responsive to your customer on the phone. The effect of this can be almost startling—in a decidedly positive fashion—to your customer, and the technologies for these tasks are readily available. In fact, both are probably in use in your business already. Using them together is a relatively simple undertaking, but one that yields impressive results.

More Ambitious Uses for the Phone

A more sophisticated use of the telephone involves self-service applications. Self-service applications are software programs that allow a customer on a touchtone phone to perform certain functions that otherwise might require the intervention of one of your employees. For example, many banks now allow their customers to perform functions like checking account balances or transferring funds over the phone.

Such tasks are not trivial undertakings and will involve a significant investment in the installation and customized implementation of enabling software. Also, many self-service applications can be handled more effectively over the Internet. Most important is that self-service phone applications should not be deployed in a way that precludes your customers from getting assistance from your employees when they want it or need it. (Chapter 15 will delve into the principles for effectively deploying self-service.)

Those caveats aside, self-service telephone applications

Parting Thoughts on Using the Phone Effectively

Customers on the phone can tell when your employees are smiling. Employees usually don't believe this. Even when they're persuaded that it's true, they often feel too embarrassed to break into a big smile before speaking with a customer on the phone. Your challenge as a manager is to help your employees overcome this reluctance because—believe it or not—a smile from your employee really can make a difference in the perceived quality of phone interactions for your customer.

Make it a game. Or make it a challenge. Just find a way to get your employees to consistently smile when they're on the phone with your customers.

can, for some businesses, represent a meaningful step toward killer customer care.

Looking Ahead

In the next chapter, you're going to learn one of the biggest, best-kept customer care secrets anywhere, one that's used by the best customer care companies in a wide variety of different industries. You're going to learn how to build entertainment—a hidden hallmark of killer customer care—into your customer's experiences with your business.

BUILD ENTERTAINMENT INTO YOUR CUSTOMERS' EXPERIENCE

GIVING CUSTOMERS A GOOD TIME

Most people, even if they aren't fully aware of it, are looking for fun in whatever they do. This includes when they are shopping, even for necessities.

So here's the point (one you may not have considered, either). Entertainment is an absolutely critical aspect of killer customer care, but it's one that receives very little attention. Whether your business engages in business-to-business transactions or deals with individual consumers, your ability to enhance your more conventional customer care efforts with an element of entertainment can have a dramatic impact on your customers' satisfaction with your company.

Chances are, up until now, you haven't spent much time thinking about the entertainment value your business offers. Before you're through with this chapter, though, you'll see your customers' experience with your business from a new and different perspective.

Entertainment: The Secret Customer Care Strategy

The fact that a company like Disney would build entertainment value into its customers' experience doesn't surprise anyone. In fact, it's expected. After all, Disney is an entertainment company. But if you think entertainment companies are the only ones that take advantage of the customer-pleasing value of entertainment, consider these few bits of data.

- **Southwest Airlines** is one of the few consistently profitable operations in the entire airline industry. Whereas its approach to flying is unique in a number of ways, many of its passengers consistently mention the friendliness and humor of its flight attendants and other personnel. It's not uncommon for the standard safety announcements on a Southwest flight to be accompanied by chuckles and even laughter.

- All of **Chef Emeril Lagasse**'s popular restaurants offer a dinner selection called *degustation*. It is a six-course sampling of an ever changing variety of menu options and requires the participation of the entire table. Each course is ceremoniously brought to the table by a phalanx of servers whose movements are so tightly coordinated that they seem to be choreographed.

- **Best Buy** sells consumer electronics. But the atmosphere in its stores often startles first-time customers. Each store is visually overwhelming, with bright lights, open spaces, lots of color, and incredible amounts of merchandise displayed everywhere.

- **Microsoft** regularly embellishes its new product introductions with glitz and glamor, attributes not usually associated with business productivity software. Celebrities ranging from Jay Leno to The

What People Like to Hear

A cursory review of the world of business speakers shows that year after year, the most highly paid speakers—the ones rated most highly by their "hard-nosed" business audiences—are seldom the speakers who present the best researched, most thoroughly documented analyses of business trends or procedures. Instead, the speakers who consistently please their audiences are the ones whose delivery is entertaining and usually amusing.

Years ago, this point was driven home to an aspiring professional seminar leader who had spent months crafting a presentation for business audiences that meticulously and thoroughly explained the intricacies of the topic he was covering. After repeatedly racking up mediocre results while trying to market follow-up seminars to his clients, the speaker sought the advice of a colleague who was a popular seminar leader in a similar market.

When his friend told him that his material was too dry, this would-be speaker's frustration was palpable as he wondered out loud, "What will it take? Do I have to do a stand-up act and make them all laugh?"

"Only if you want to get paid," was his friend's candid reply.

Rolling Stones have been involved in various new product introductions from the Redmond, Washington, software giant.

Clearly, the customer care value of entertainment is appreciated by a wide variety of companies that are not in the entertainment business, per se. Or, perhaps a more useful take on this phenomenon is that, in one way or another, *every* company is in the entertainment business. The fact that customers of all sorts value entertainment comes as a shock to many businesspeople who can't find any data among their surveys and focus groups to document this rarely discussed tendency. But there's little question that it exists. (One suspects that it's the same sort of phenomenon as reading *The National Enquirer*. Obviously, a lot of people do it but it's difficult to find anyone who will actually admit to it.)

The bottom line for you and your business is that you will get much closer to achieving killer customer care if you can find ways to build entertainment value into your interactions with customers. A few places to start:

- Entertaining employee performances
- Entertaining environments
- Entertaining product displays

Entertaining Employee Performances

This is a highly effective technique for interjecting entertainment value into almost any customer interaction, but it's also one that is easy to get wrong. There is often a fine line between being entertaining and being annoying. It's one that even professional entertainers cross periodically, so the odds of an employee crossing the line inadvertently are considerable. Still, the upside of getting it right makes the risk one that's worthwhile, especially since you can take steps to increase the likelihood of getting it right.

Cultivating entertaining employees begins with your hiring process. It's easier for a naturally outgoing individual to be entertaining than one who is introverted. When you're filling positions that might require an employee to "perform" for your customers (in the show-business sense of that word), look for natural performers, candidates who come into the job interview smiling and who are on the edge of their chairs the entire time they're talking to you.

Once you've filled your positions with the right people, consider how those employees will interact with your customers. In many businesses, customers will interact with employees relatively infrequently. A company like Southwest Airlines, for example, might only see an average customer once or twice a year. If that's the case in your business, consider providing employees with a script or, at least, a series of conversation or presentation elements that are reliably funny.

The most gifted performers in the world work from scripts; there's nothing inappropriate about your employees doing the same thing. Scripted interactions have three important advantages.

1. Over time you'll be able to develop scripts that consistently produce the desired results.
2. Your employees will be able to approach their "performances" with a high degree of confidence.
3. The use of scripts will minimize the chance of an employee inadvertently offending customers with an inappropriate remark.

A final observation about entertaining employee performances: they don't happen without work and practice. Give your employees plenty of opportunity to hone their presentations and receive constructive criticism from their colleagues—and from you. Consider sending them to a stand-up comedy class at your local community college! It's not easy, and it might take time, but if you can get this right, you'll have taken a step toward killer customer care that will be extremely difficult for your competitors to duplicate.

Entertaining Environments

It's happened to you, although you might not have realized at the time that what you were seeing was entertainment. You walked into a store or office, stopped, looked around, and said to yourself "Wow!"

There is an infinite number of ways to achieve this effect, and there isn't a cookie-cutter approach that works in every business environment. Sometimes, the right effect is one that is "over the top"—perhaps downright gaudy. Other times, the best approach is understated but quietly opulent. Still other times, the most effective environment is one that is "busy" and engaging.

Start by deciding on the effect you want to achieve or the mood you want to create. Your approach will depend on the nature of your product or service and on the nature of the customer you're seeking to impress. For inspiration, think about those times in your own experience when you entered a business and said "Wow!" What caught your attention and impressed you? How can you incorporate some of those elements into your own store or office?

Once you have a mental image of the effect you want to achieve, identify where your customers enter your business. Those locations are the most important ones for creating the "wow" effect. If you're successful in achieving your design objectives at these locations, then the impact you create will persist, even as your customer moves to less impressive vantage points. If you can't achieve a wow effect at the point your customer enters your store or business, it is going to be exceedingly difficult to do so further on.

Entertaining Product Displays

If you haven't done this lately, take a 7- or 8-year-old child with you to the supermarket sometime, —preferably to one of the major chain stores that pay attention to effective merchandising. Accompany the child to the breakfast cereal aisle, ask him or her to pick one out, and watch what happens. Just make sure you have plenty of time because it's probably going to take a while. Your diminutive research subject will more than likely be completely mesmerized by the selection, taking it all in with a degree of care and attention that surpasses what you might observe at most art museums.

Before you decide that children are uniquely susceptible to entertaining product displays, pay a visit to the high-end television section of a large consumer electronics store with

As impressive as an entertaining environment can be, it shouldn't take precedence over utility. In the pursuit of killer customer care, entertainment value is an enabling factor, but your ability to elegantly deliver a result for your customer should be your overriding design consideration.

a 30- or 40-year-old male. If you do this soon after your experiment in the cereal aisle with the 8-year-old, you'll recognize immediately that look in his eyes. And while they would probably articulate it differently, the underlying reaction of both shoppers would be, "That was fun!"

How do you create entertaining product displays? Basically, you can follow the guidelines we just explored for creating entertaining environments. In addition to those suggestions, though, entertaining product displays also follow that uniquely American principle: *nothing succeeds like excess*. In other words, when it comes to displays more is usually better.

Entertainment by its very nature is not a quantifiable element. As is the case with so many aspects of killer customer care, your ability to implement this successfully is as much art as it is science. You're off to a good start, however, in merely recognizing that you should seek entertainment value.

Once you have that nugget of understanding, your best course of action is to follow the guidelines discussed here, experiment liberally, and watch carefully for what works. Of course, it's won't be simple or straightforward. But once you achieve it, it will absolutely be worth the time and effort it took to get there.

Looking Ahead

One "can't miss" method for delivering killer customer care is to make sure your customers walk away from their interactions with more than they expected. In the next chapter, we're going to examine some techniques for consistently achieving that highly desirable result without incurring exorbitant costs or expending superhuman efforts. As you'll see in Chapter 13, it's mostly a question of insight, planning, and paying attention.

EXCEED YOUR CUSTOMERS' EXPECTATIONS

GIVE THEM MORE THAN THEY EXPECT

I n Chapter 5, you learned one of the most important principles of killer customer care, The Delta Principle. Let's take a moment to review this foundational principle.

The quality of your customers' experience is not a direct result of the objective quality of your products or services. Instead, customers' satisfaction is a more a function of how closely their experience with your business conforms with their expectations.

It's easy to see how this fundamental principle could work, in theory. If your budget were unlimited and profitability wasn't a consideration, you could use it to unfailingly achieve killer customer care in your interactions with customers. As we saw in Chapter 5, the key doesn't necessarily lie in the objective level of service you provide or in the quality of your product as it might be measured by an impartial observer. It lies in consistently exceeding the expectations your customers bring to your dealings.

A Small "Delta" Makes a Big Difference

In practice, though, it's natural to worry that constantly exceeding customers' expectations might be prohibitively expensive, particularly in industries that are especially competitive or operate on low margins. If that is your concern, then I have great news that will alleviate your worries. The effectiveness of your efforts to exceed your customers' expectations is not determined by the degree to which your customers' expectations are exceeded. Instead, it's determined by the consistency with which your performance outstrips their expectations.

In other words, it's not necessary for you to undertake any grand, expensive gestures to achieve killer customer care. It is merely necessary that you consistently undertake the kinds of small gestures that can bring a smile to your customer's face.

Modest Gestures Make a Difference

A grand gesture can impress a customer temporarily, but it can also produce one of two reactions, neither of which is particularly positive. One possible reaction is when it appears the economics of the original transaction were so badly skewed against the customer that you could afford to be extravagant. Your customer might then see your grand gesture as an indication that he's paying too much to do business with you.

The other, more likely, reaction is that the grand gesture is nice but not a part of your business relationship that you could sustain. As a result, the customer might be grateful but not necessarily motivated to reward your business with the kind of loyalty that killer customer care is supposed to produce.

Modest gestures that exceed your customer's expectations, on the other hand, are perceived by your customer to be highly sustainable. As a result, those gestures will do precisely what they were designed to do: instill in your customer an abiding loyalty to your business and a marked disinclination to experiment with your competitors.

Low-Cost, High-Impact Opportunities to Exceed Expectations

So let's take a look at seven specific strategies for exceeding the expectations your customers bring to your business. All of these strategies are designed to be implemented at little or no cost to you while simultaneously creating a considerable impact on your customer and her perception of your business. The seven strategies for exceeding customer expectations are:

- Add information-based value
- Upgrade services at no extra charge (when possible)
- Bundle in opportunities from complementary businesses
- Include frequent buyer bonuses and surprises
- Take a few extra moments
- Get personal
- Express an interest in the outcome

Add Information-Based Value

An enormous disparity exists between the value of relevant, desirable information for your customer and the cost for you to provide that information. (The value/cost disparity for information is even greater than the value/cost disparity for bottled "designer" water—a genuinely remarkable ratio!) The significance of this fact is that you can use information to create enormous value for your customer with little or no adverse impact on your cost of sales or operating margins.

There are many ways you can deliver the information your customer wants. Booklets, Web sites, audiocassettes, and seminars are just a few of the more popular ones. Home Depot is a worthwhile case study of a business that strategically deploys pertinent, desirable information in order to add value and exceed the customers' expectations.

Think about your products and services and about the customers who buy them. What information are they likely to find useful or helpful? Once you've identified the information that's most likely to add value, then consider the various options at your disposal for making it available to your customer. Bundling helpful information in with your offering not only enhances the relationship between you and your customer, it also increases the perceived value of *all* your products and services. It is an important tool in your quest to create killer customer care.

Upgrade Services at No Extra Charge (When Possible)

Many of your company's upgraded offerings carry with them additional costs that would make you understandably reluctant to offer them to customers for no additional charge. Some upgrades, though, don't fall into this category, and when that's the case, you can exceed your customer's expectations by strategically offering upgraded products or levels of service for no aditional charge.

Let's take a look at an admittedly exaggerated example to illustrate this concept. You operate a hotel in a small market. It's 12:45 A.M. in the middle of the week, it's pouring down rain outside, and the last flight into the local airport landed more than an hour ago. Your property is somewhat less than packed after a last-minute cancellation by the Knights of Pitheous convention.

Through the front door stumbles the last remaining reservation on your books, a family of four that includes an obviously cranky 3-year-old and his even more cranky baby brother. They look like they've been driving for several hours to reach the standard room with two double beds that they've booked.

Those tired customers would probably be very happy if your desk clerk could just get them into their room relatively quickly with as little fuss as possible. The imperatives of killer customer care, however, suggest that it makes sense to go beyond that merely adequate level of performance. Your employee should not hesitate to upgrade this family to a suite, at no additional charge. The business will incur no extra expense, but it exceeds the customer's expectations in a manner sure to be remembered (and discussed) for days and weeks to come.

Does your business have opportunities to upgrade your customers without diminishing your profitability? If so, then it makes sense to train your employees to find them.

Bundle in Opportunities from Complementary Businesses

Some businesses sell to a customer base that is broad and undifferentiated. By contrast, many businesses attract a customer base that is distinct and has an identifiable profile. That profile might be demographic (single men between the ages of 18 and 24) or it might be based on affinity (vintage Corvette owners). If your business falls into the latter category, chances are you have an opportunity to exceed your customers' expectations that you might not have considered.

If your customer base is distinct, there's a good chance other, noncompeting businesses spend a great deal of money to market their products and services to the same customer base. The opportunity lies in creating a relationship with one or more of those businesses to benefit customers.

Let's say your business specializes in the sale and installation of customer relationship management software for small and medium-sized businesses. Who else might be selling to that marketplace in a way that is completely noncompetitive with what you're offering? An office products dealer might fit the bill. Now, what does that dealer pay in marketing costs to get a new customer in the door? Let's ballpark the figure at somewhere between $50 and $100. If that's the case, then the dealer might be willing to extend a special offer to your clients in the form of a coupon for $35 off their initial purchase. Your customers win because they save $35 on merchandise they are likely to buy anyway. The office products dealer wins by acquiring a new customer at a substantial discount from his usual customer acquisition cost. And you win, of course, because you have created value that allows you to exceed your customers' expectations.

Include Frequent Buyer Bonuses and Surprises

You no doubt have a customer information system in place that tracks your customers along with other important information such as what they've purchased and how often they buy from you. (If you don't, then go back and review Chapter 8.) This system should certainly be able to help you identify your "frequent buyers, " who by definition, are the 20 percent of your customers who contribute 80 percent of your sales volume and probably an even greater percentage of your profits.

These customers deserve special treatment—and you can certainly afford to give it to them. If you think you can't, then just think ponder for a moment how expensive it would be to replace someone from this elite group if he or she bolts to one of your competitors. Considering the impersonal business environment that exists in most industries today, chances are good that special treatment isn't something that these customers expect.

Direct Costs

Consider what might happen if the manager of your store approached one of your frequent buyers while she was still at the checkout counter and said, "I just wanted you to know that we have appreciated all the confidence you've shown us in giving us your business over the years. You might not be aware of it, but this is your 50th purchase here, and we appreciate your business as much now as we appreciated your first purchase two years ago."

That small gesture would dramatically exceed your customer's expectations—and it would certainly be something that she would describe as killer customer care.

All of these factors combine to make this a wonderful opportunity to exceed your customer's expectations. And, in the process, you can tie that customer to your business more tightly than ever before.

Use your imagination to develop unexpected bonuses and surprises for your frequent buyers. You might decide to create something outrageous, but something simple and understated can work just as well.

Take a Few Extra Moments

Frequent buyers aren't the only ones who would appreciate a thoughtful gesture. In a commercial environment that has grown increasingly impersonal over the years, even a few extra moments' worth of attention from one of your employees can make all the difference in the world.

A busy retail setting with lots of customers waiting is obviously not the best place to implement this particular bit of advice. On the other hand, most customer interactions provide ample opportunity for this kind of added attentiveness.

Here's a phrase that ought to be in the repertoire of every person in your organization: "Is there anything else I can help you with today?" It doesn't seem like much, but it's probably more than your customers are getting elsewhere. It's the quickest, most inexpensive way there is for you to find out how to exceed your customer's expectations.

Get Personal

Whenever possible, have your employees introduce themselves. Sporting a name tag is a good start, but it isn't quite the same thing. And, whenever possible, follow the guidelines we covered in Chapter 7 about using your customer's name.

Have your employees make it clear to your customer that this transaction is unique and special, that it is not just the next product of some corporate cookie cutter.

Express an Interest in the Outcome

Finally, have your employees make it clear to the customer that they are interested in the outcome of any transaction or interaction. In a southeast supermarket chain, the cashiers are trained to provide a sunny "Hello" to the stores' customers when they reach the checkout counter, followed by the question, "Did you find everything you were looking for today?"

There are a number of questions your employees might use, depending on the nature of your business: "Is that what you were expecting?" or "Does this look like it will work for you?" are just a couple. The object is for your employees to convey to your customer the message that they don't take the customer's satisfaction for granted, that they want to doublecheck to make sure the result is satisfactory.

Looking Ahead

Killer customer care often comes down to what football coaches refer to as "blocking and tackling." This phrase has a specific meaning on the football field but is often used more broadly to describe the fundamental elements of a task that ought to be done flawlessly, every time. Keeping commitments to customers is one of those fundamental elements, and we're going to examine it in Chapter 14.

KEEP COMMITMENTS TO CUSTOMERS

DO WHAT YOU SAY YOU WILL DO ◀

When it happens, it hardly seems like a big transgression. It's the kind of thing that could happen to just about anyone. It's probably even happened to you.

You're just about to walk into a meeting when your phone rings. You're tempted to let it roll over into your voice-mail system but, for some reason, you decide to pick up the call. Bad decision.

It's the customer from that small deal you closed last week. He apologizes for bothering you but says he needs to ask a favor. Would you mind faxing over another copy of the paperwork? The copy he took with him is sitting on his desk in Minneapolis, and he needs a copy at corporate in Omaha for an important presentation to his boss's boss in the morning.

No problem, you tell him. You jot down the fax number on the corner of your calendar and promise to take care of it as soon as you get out of the meeting—which is just about to start.

The meeting runs long and is more than a little contentious. By the time you get out, faxing the paperwork is the farthest thing from your mind. You never give it another thought—until the following afternoon....

Sound familiar? Of course it does. Very few people in business haven't committed that sort of slipup once or twice in their careers. But it's not the end of the world, you tell yourself. In the overall scheme of things, commitments like that are relatively small, aren't they? And as long as you take care of the big things, you're OK, aren't you? After all, it's the big things customers consider when they're evaluating your customer care performance, right?

Besides, your daily calendar is jammed. It's probably busier than ever before, and the same is likely true for all of your employees. Isn't that also part of the nature of today's business environment? Isn't it true that little things fall through the cracks all the times these days? Isn't that just how the business world works today?

A Commitment Is a Commitment

If you think the little things don't count (or don't count very much), then consider this: in today's competitive business environment, just about *everyone* gets the big things right, at least most of the time. Customers simply have too many choices today to allow genuinely poor performers to stay in business. Today's business world is relentlessly Darwinian. In the realm of customer care, standards of performance that once constituted killer customer care are now merely adequate, and ones that were adequate just a short time ago are no longer even acceptable. Today, your challenge is to make sure your level of performance—the level of performance achieved by everyone in your organization—meets and exceeds today's standards.

How does all of this relate to this issue of small commitments to customers sometimes falling through the cracks? Well, without getting too abstract, let's start to answer that question with a quick look at what a commitment is and what constitutes a commitment.

"Commitment" means "the act of binding yourself to a course of action." In other words, it's a promise to do something. It is worth noting, though, what's absent from this definition. There's nothing in the definition about the relative importance of the action to which one commits one's self. There aren't "big" commitments and "small" commitments—only commitments. As our friends in the world of technology might put it, commitment is a binary value. Either it's on or it's off.

Even more important, there is nothing in the definition that suggests a commitment depends on the relative importance of the action as retroactively determined by the person making the commitment. Once a commitment is made to a customer, there is no option to look back and decide it just wasn't that big of a deal.

From your customers' standpoint, a commitment is an indication to them that they can count on something getting done. Period. Sworn oaths or written contracts are not necessary in order to create a commitment. Even an off-hand remark can do the trick. "I'll take care if it" or "Don't worry about it" are the sorts of remarks that can be made without giving them a great deal of thought, but they can convey a loud and clear message to a customer.

Customers Value Commitments (Even Small Ones)

Here's the part of this analysis that's critical. Your customers highly value the commitments made to them, even ones that are apparently minor or insignificant. Moreover, a commitment that seems small or insignificant to you might very well be important to your customer. Whiffing on those "small" commitments can undermine all of your other efforts to achieve killer customer care.

Consider the case of a loan officer who specializes in homeowner refinancing. All day, every day, she's working with homeowners who are refinancing their mortgages. There is nothing about the refinancing process that is unknown to her, and there are no little hiccups or glitches in the process that she hasn't dealt with over and over again.

The homeowner on the other end of the phone, however, looks at refinancing from a completely different perspective. For him, it's a strange and frightening process: Strange because he's never done it before and because it involves a tremendous number of unfamiliar documents that he doesn't understand very well; frightening because it is the largest single financial transaction he's undertaken in his life.

Imagine, then, a brief, throwaway remark made by the loan officer to the homeowner: "I'll take a look at everything and give you a call back tomorrow morning to review where we stand."

When the next morning comes, our intrepid loan officer finds herself with a few unexpected fires to put out. The phone call she had intended to make to review the status of the homeowner's application slips (unavoidably, she might claim) to the bottom of her priority list. In her mind, it's no big deal. The application looks good and, what the heck, there really isn't that much to talk about. She rolls up her sleeves to attack the work in front of her, resolving to get back to this particular homeowner after lunch or tomorrow morning, at the latest. No problem.

Cut to scene two, 11:40 A.M. at the kitchen table of the homeowner. He's been distinctly fidgety since 10:00 A.M., and now he is downright edgy. What is going wrong? Is there a problem with his credit? Did he do something wrong on the paperwork? Why didn't he let his brother-in-law look everything over before he sent it in?

You get the picture. The loan officer clearly did not consider her remark to be a "commitment" when she made it. She barely gave it any thought. The customer, however, saw her comment in an entirely different light.

Fail-Safe Systems for Commitments

The procedure for making certain this doesn't happen in your business is straightforward and twofold. First, make sure that your employees understand the importance of commitments and what sorts of remarks constitute a commitment in the minds of your customers. Your employees don't intend to mislead your customers. They're simply looking at the interaction with your customer from a somewhat different perspective. If they take a moment to think about how a transaction might feel to your customer, they'll develop a much better track record for meeting commitments.

The second part of the process for reliably meeting commitments is to immediately put those commitments into a fail-safe system in order to make sure they receive the follow-up attention they need. For most of your employees, this will mean using software that manages their contacts and activities. For many of them, this part of the procedure will be relatively easy because they're already using this type of software to keep track of the "big" things, like appointments.

For these employees, a fail-safe system for following up on commitments will happen when they simply lower the threshold for which events to enter into the system. Your sales organization is probably using software like this already. Some of the more popular products for managing contacts and activities are Outlook, ACT!, and Goldmine.

For those employees who are not yet using this type of system but use a computer regularly, this type of software is a great investment and will pay for itself readily by facilitating levels of killer customer care that are difficult to achieve without it.

For your employees who don't use a computer regularly, there are several paper-based systems that will achieve similar results. Day-Timers and Franklin Planners are two of the more popular ones. Even a "homegrown" paper-based system can work well.

The key to keeping commitments to customers is to make sure your employees enter *every* commitment into whichever system they're using, computer- or paper-based, and then check that system regularly so nothing is forgotten or overlooked.

Backup Procedures for When Things Go Wrong

Even the best-designed systems are sometimes subject to unanticipated glitches that are beyond anyone's control. And even the best of intentions on the part of your employees will sometimes be undermined by circumstances that are unforeseen and unavoidable. What happens then?

The answer is to provide your customer a backup plan in advance. Often, this will mean having your employee give him the name, phone, and e-mail address of an alternate contact who will be able to help him if there's a problem or if the employee is unreachable for some reason. Depending on the nature of the commitment, your employee also could provide the customer with alternative procedures that would create the same result, either online or via the telephone. (We'll look at the subject of self-service in the next chapter.)

What's important is to make sure your customer is not without alternatives if there is an unavoidable problem that prevents you or an employee from following through on a commitment in a timely manner.

Keeping Commitments Starts at the Top

The last thing to keep in mind about commitments to customers is that your organization's willingness and determination to follow through is an attribute that—like so many other characteristics of a business—starts at the top. If employees sense that your company's senior (or even middle) managers are cavalier about keeping commitments they've made, then those employees will behave in a similar fashion. On the other hand, if they see managers regard a customer commitment as inviolable, then they will follow suit.

Like so many other aspects of killer customer care, the culture of the company (as we saw in Chapter 2) will influence the results you achieve more than the details of the policies, procedures, and systems you put into place.

Looking Ahead

We've already explored the concept of giving customers the tools they need to get the information want. One of the most interesting customer care discoveries of the last three decades is the realization that, in many instances, self-service is the service option customers prefer. In the next chapter, we'll examine why that is so and explore techniques you can use to put your customer in control.

PUT YOUR CUSTOMER IN CONTROL

Here's a story that—if you were born before 1960—will cause you to look back on an earlier time with amusement and a certain amount of wistfulness. (On the other hand, if you were born after 1960, it will probably confirm your suspicion that everyone over 45 is clueless about technology and its uses.)

The first automated teller machines began to appear in the lobbies of banks in the early 1970s. As is usually the case with the introduction of any new, disruptive technology, there were widely varying opinions about its prospects for success. In the ensuing debate about the efficacy of the ATM, two sides emerged with dramatically different predictions about whether or not the public would embrace this new approach to banking.

One side predicted widespread success based on the convenience the new machines would offer customers, particularly the ability to take care of business after regular banking hours, which were even more inconvenient then than they are today. The other side of the debate held that the very idea of these machines was ridiculous.

Why, the skeptics asked, would a customer ever consider using one of these machines when he could walk inside and conduct business in person with a real, live teller?

Of course, the proponents of ATM technology turned out to be correct but for reasons that went beyond those that dominated the debate at the time. The naysayers' arguments seem silly now with the benefit of hindsight, but it's worth noting that both sides of the debate missed a factor that turned out to be at least as important as convenience in driving the acceptance of ATMs. Simply put, customers want *their* fingers—not yours—on the "Enter" key for their transactions.

The proliferation of ATMs was a harbinger of things to come. We now know that the self-service imperative has become one of the most significant customer care factors in today's business environment. In fact, for many customers, the availability of a self-service option is an absolute requisite for killer customer care.

The Various Self-Service Tools at Your Disposal

There are three important options at your disposal for effectively extending self-service capabilities to your customers.

- *The Web.* This is the most powerful and most versatile of the options that are available to you. In addition, it is often the most convenient one for your customers. It is also worth noting that it can be relatively inexpensive to deploy. All of the capabilities described in this chapter—and more—are achievable with Web technology.
- *Self-service phone applications.* We've already seen these in Chapter 11. The phone's great advantage is

its ubiquity. Its most significant limitation is that it's not readily suited to working with alphabetical (as opposed to numeric) data. It is a useful option when the number of options and alternatives in a self-service system is finite and when your customers can be identified with a unique account number. Self-service phone applications and Web-based self-service options are not mutually exclusive and are often deployed in parallel.

- *Specialized in-store tools.* Many businesses provide self-service options for their customers that are specially designed or highly specialized in their functioning. Target Department Stores, for example, place price scanners throughout their stores, allowing customers to check the pricing for any bar-coded merchandise.

Elements of a Well-Designed Self-Service Option

Self-service is a powerful tool for achieving killer customer care when it's implemented properly, but it can frustrate and even anger your customers when it isn't. There are three factors that you should consider in designing and implementing any self-service option.

- System reliability
- User interface
- A feedback loop

System Reliability

Looking back at the example of ATMs, we know that skepticism about the reliability of the machines and the accuracy of the transactions was a factor that impeded their adoption during the first few years of their existence. The rule here is pretty straightforward. Customers will avoid a self-service system they don't trust.

They don't want to spend time entering an order, for example, only to have it returned for some nitpicky reason. If they suspect that might happen, they'd rather enlist the aid of one of your employees (on the phone or in person) to get it done properly. This reliability rule is doubly true because it also impacts customer convenience.

User Interface

This is a term that refers to how your customers interact with your self-service systems. A user interface can be friendly and intuitive, or it can be difficult and confusing. The ideal user interface needs little instruction or explanation and allows the user to accomplish various tasks with a minimum amount of time and effort. Usually, there's an inverse relationship between a system's complexity and the elegance of its user interface.

It's often assumed that graphic elements make a user interface easier, although that's not necessarily true. Words can often be more straightforward and understandable than obscure icons. Customers will be more likely to use *any* kind of self-service system if it has a friendly and intuitive user interface.

A Feedback Loop

This is an element of the user interface, but it's so important—and so often overlooked—that it merits a separate mention. A feedback loop tells users whether something they were trying to accomplish either worked or didn't. If you were in an elevator, for example, how would it feel if you pressed the button to go to the seventh floor and there was no light on the button to indicate that your "request" was received? You'd have no idea whether or not the ele-

> *One Southeast supermarket chain features self-service checkout lines that allow customers to scan their own orders. Over time, the scanning equipment has proven to be unreliable. Understandably, most of the chain's customers have given up and chosen to wait in line for a regular checkout clerk rather than take a chance on wasting their time with the temperamental machines.*
>
> *The self-service checkout lines, as a result, are typically empty. This is a surefire indication, by the way, that the self-service system has failed!*

Poorly Designed Self-Service

In most supermarkets, the credit card machines at checkout are an example of a self-service option that suffers from a chronically poor user interface. Just figuring how to swipe the card in order to get started can be a challenge—and it gets worse from there.

The weakness of the design is betrayed by the fact that many cashiers immediately begin coaching customers on how to use the machine as soon as they pull out a credit card. This is a sign that customers almost always wind up having problems or, at least, questions about how to use the system—another indication of a poorly designed self-service system.

vator got the message to take you to the seventh floor. You'd have no feedback.

When a customer is using a self-service system, he or she needs feedback that any choices made during the use of the system were made correctly and accepted by the system. That's what a feedback loop provides.

The "When" and "How" of Deploying Self-Service Effectively

How can you take advantage of your customers' innate inclination for self-service to achieve killer customer care in your business? Start by looking for elements of customer interaction where your employees don't add any particular value. (As you explore this issue, you might well identify places where employees actually interfere with the task at hand but can't figure out how to get out of the way!) Also, identify situations where your customers regularly seem to become impatient with your employees or where they're forced to wait for some employee intervention to do something they could otherwise accomplish themselves.

Below is a discussion of some ideas and principles that will be useful as you evaluate the best ways to implement self-service options in your business.

Let your customers "own" their customer profiles. If you're keeping records of contact information and other useful customer information, why not get them involved in both the creation and maintenance of that information? On a Web site, implementing this principle is a given, but you can just as easily do it in a sales office or store by making terminals available that will allow a customer to create and/or edit their profiles.

Give customers access to as much of your information as possible. You might, for example, deploy terminals in your stores that will allow your customers to see what's in stock in the back room. If you have more than one store, let them see if an item that's out of stock in one location might be available elsewhere. Online or in-store, give your customers the ability to check prices, search for specials, obtain volume discount information, or view manufacturers' rebate availability.

Give customers access to information about their orders and accounts. If a customer has an order pending with your company, there's no reason why that customer should have to talk to one of your employees to check the status of that order. Use the Web to give your customers the ability to place special orders without the help of an associate. Let them perform maintenance functions on their credit accounts with your business, including tasks such as checking their credit limits or requesting a higher credit line.

Let customers manage their incentive awards online. One large hotel chain insists that its customers request a paper certificate in order to redeem free nights earned through its frequent guest program. That sort of bureaucratic hurdle is perceived by customers as ridiculous. If you offer something like incentives, allow your customers to redeem them online.

Let your offline customers shop online. Circuit City provides an example of this principle that is well worth studying. Circuit City customers have the option of shopping online (including the ability to query the local store's inventory in real-time to make sure the desired merchandise is in stock) and then picking up their order in person.

Let your customers do their own paperwork. If your business requires that paperwork be filled out, get your employees out of the middle and allow your customers to enter their information into your systems directly. Your customers will be happier, and your employees will be free to engage in activities that genuinely add value. As an added benefit, the information in your systems will likely be far more accurate.

The Last (and Most Important) Word on Self-Service

As you explore ways in which to use self-service options to achieve killer customer care, keep in mind a final principle that is critically important. For all of their power and appeal, self-service systems must always accommodate a customer's decision—at any time and for any reason—to

Why Self-Service Fails

Too many businesses fail in deploying self-service options because they approach them as a vehicle for lowering costs rather than as a tool for empowering customers. There is an almost Zen-like paradox to self-service. If your focus in deploying a self-service option is on lowering costs, you may well wind up with a system that neither lowers costs nor improves customer care.

But if you focus on creating a system that works for your customers (including allowing them to opt for personalized attention when they want it), you will almost certainly succeed in achieving killer customer care *and* lowering your costs.

opt out of the system and request help from an employee. Self-service ought to be an empowering option for your customers, not a restriction of their options. If it's perceived as the latter, it will likely meet with resistance and, ultimately, failure.

Looking Ahead

Several times so far, we've referenced the use of a customer information system. In the next chapter, we'll explore that system in depth. In Chapter 16, you'll learn about the workings of a customer information system and the sometimes startling information you can extract from one—if you know how.

USE YOUR CUSTOMER INFORMATION EFFECTIVELY

PROFITING FROM KNOWING YOUR CUSTOMERS ◀

O bviously, your choice to invest in this book was wise. Ostensibly, you did so for reasons other than the fact that it will look great on your bookshelf (although it certainly will). More likely, you did it so you could learn as much as possible about providing a superior level of care for your customers, a level we have referred to throughout this book as killer customer care.

But as helpful as this book might be (and, obviously, it was conceived and designed to be as helpful as possible), it cannot provide you with specific information about how to deliver killer customer care to your particular customers, in your particular marketplace. There is only one conclusive source where you can turn regularly for consistently reliable information about your customers. Of course, that source of information is your customers themselves.

This book provides guidelines you can follow and suggests general strategies and techniques you can use, but when it comes to filling in the blanks with the specifics that will allow you to apply those strategies and techniques to your business, the only place to get that information is from your customers.

There are several ways to get the information you'll need, and you should absolutely use all of them. A couple of general methods involve getting your customers to tell you what they think and want in a variety of different areas. We'll examine those approaches in Chapters 24 and 25. In this chapter, though, we're going to explore ways to extract information, not from what your customers *say*, but instead from who they *are* and from what they *do*. And that kind information can only be gleaned from a customer information system or database.

We've alluded to your customer information system several times already. Now, it's time to get more specific about exactly what it is and what you can learn from it.

The Basics

As the term implies, a customer information system is a repository for information you collect about your customers over time. This information is accumulated and maintained by software known as customer relationship management (CRM) software. A comprehensive review of CRM software is well outside the scope of this book, but the category is a broad one and encompasses options suitable for business of all different sizes, of all different types (e.g., retail, professional services, etc.), and in any industry you can imagine.

Your customer information system will help you accumulate and manage three types of information about your customers:

1. Identifying and demographic information
2. Transactional information
3. Information about nontransactional interactions

The size of the investment required to implement a CRM solution can vary dramatically, depending on the functions you need and the number of employees in your company who will access the system. Implemented properly, a CRM solution can deliver a respectable return on your investment by increasing sales productivity and lowering your cost of selling. And CRM software can help you understand your customers better, a prerequisite for delivering killer customer care.

Identifying and Demographic Information

The most fundamental information about your customer can be labeled identifying and demographic information. If your business sells primarily to individual consumers, you'll begin by collecting their names, mailing addresses, phone numbers, and e-mail addresses. It can also be very helpful to record how your business and your customer came into contact. (Did your customer answer an ad? If so, which ad? In which medium? Did they hear about your business somewhere else? Did you find them? If so, how?)

If your business sells to other businesses, you'll want to include organizational information about those businesses. Where are the corporate offices? Are there any branch offices you need to track? You'll also want to record information about the various individuals at the business with whom you have contact. Do you sell into a variety of different industries? If so, you'll want to track the industry of each of your customers. Do you sell to companies of different sizes? If that's the case, design your information system to the size of each of your various customers as well.

Below is a quick list of some ideas for the kinds of information that might be valuable to you.

Information About Business Customers
- Industry (SIC code)
- Number of employees
- Approximate gross sales volume
- Ownership (public or private)
- Business type (retail, manufacturer, etc.)
- Referral source
- Purchasing history

Information About Individual Consumers
- Gender

- Marital status
- Parenthood status
- Home ownership status
- Hobbies
- Referral source
- Pet ownership status

Transactional Information

This category encompasses all of your transactions with a particular customer, including service and repair calls.

Although collecting this information is straightforward enough in theory, it can be fairly challenging in practice. The difficulty lies in the fact that, for many businesses, the transactional information is created and maintained in several different systems. A company that sells business services might generate invoices from its accounting software, but service and repair invoices might be generated from an entirely different system.

It is not necessary for all of these transactions to be duplicated in your customer information system. That's the good news. The bad news is your various systems will need to "talk" to one another so you can use your CRM software to examine information about transactions that exist in other places. Depending on the technical details of your systems, that might be more difficult than it sounds.

If you are lucky enough to be designing your company's systems from the ground up, then this type of integration should be relatively easy to accomplish. (The operative word in that sentence is "relatively.") On the other hand, if you already have one or more components of an overall information architecture in place, then you may have some serious work ahead of you.

Integration Isn't Easy

Integrating systems is not for the faint of heart, nor is it wise to try to get it done "on the cheap." There is no question, though, that an investment here can pay off handsomely. At the beginning of this chapter, we noted that a customer information system will allow you to glean important insight from what your customers *do* rather than what they *say*.

With that principle in mind, remember that—for you—transactions represent the most important thing your customers *do*. You are operating at a serious disadvantage if you don't give yourself the tools to examine, review, and analyze their transactions carefully.

Information About Nontransactional Interactions

Your customer can have a number of important interactions with your business that are not transactional. Here are just a few examples:

- Complaints
- Product availability inquiries
- Requests for a proposal
- Referrals

Your ability to analyze the origin and frequency of these nontransactional interactions is tremendously important in developing and refining your killer customer care plan over time.

Getting Information into the System

Some of the information you'll want to track in your system can be entered as soon as a relationship with a customer (or potential customer) is established or when a transaction takes place, such as when a purchase is made at a retail outlet.

Direct Costs

Radio Shack has perfected the art of gathering customer basic information. When a customer makes a purchase at a Radio Shack store—even if it's something as small as a four-pack of batteries—the sales associate begins the transaction by asking the customer for his or her phone number (which, by the way, works pretty well in a consumer business as a unique identifier). If the phone number is in the company's information system, the customer's information pops up on the point-of-sale terminal and the associate continues with the transaction, which is then appended to the customer's record.

If the phone number is not already in the information system, the associate then asks the customer for his or her name and address to begin the process of creating a customer record. When making the request, the associate behaves in a matter-of-fact manner and acts as if he or she assumes the request will be honored. As a result, customer compliance in providing the information is high.

However, the company keeps its eye on the objective of killer customer care, even as it builds its customer database. A cash customer who doesn't want to disclose the informaton or be entered into the system is never forced to do so.

In nonretail situations, other methods of accumulating information can be employed. In Chapter 7, you'll recall, we touched on incentives that will encourage your customers to provide information. The specific techniques you use will depend on your business and its unique requirements. And, of course, using multiple techniques will improve your results.

After a customer record is created, additional information can be added over time. As your customer information system is integrated into your day-to-day business operations, gathering data that will be useful later on will become increasingly easier. Transactional information will append itself to a customer's record automatically. Nontransactional information, including demographic information not collected when the customer record was created, can be added as it is generated or uncovered.

Getting Information out of the System

To a certain extent, merely accumulating information can support your efforts to deliver killer customer care. If you have a well-maintained customer information system, for example, your customer will not have to endlessly repeat information such as a phone number or delivery address to your employees. That information will be in the system and need only be verified by the employee, not re-entered for every transaction.

Once you get beyond this fundamental level, you can take major steps toward killer customer care based on the information you extract from your customer information system. If you've done a good job at getting information into the system, then there are two levels at which you can use that information effectively.

The first, more basic level is to simply compile straight-forward reports. Every customer information system allows you to search through the information you've collected and sort it based on any category you want. For example, you can see how many complaints you've had about a certain product during a specified period of time. You can then scrutinize that information to determine if there is a specific category of customer who is particularly prone to that problem. Information like this will allow you to be proactive in addressing customers' concerns, rectifying problems while they are comparatively small rather than allowing them to snowball.

The second, more sophisticated level allows you to analyze information through software tools that perform analysis know as data mining. This software sifts through your information meticulously, searching for hidden relationships among the data elements that would not be

> *T*rain employees to skim a customer's record during every interaction. When the employee notices a gap in information, he or she can pick out one—and only one—item to fill in during that interaction. Have the employee choose the single most important piece of missing information. Trying to update the entire record would be time-consuming and is likely to annoy the customer. However, using this method, over time you can accumulate all of the information you want about your customers without alienating them.

apparent through more conventional analysis.

One of the most famous and instructive examples of data mining comes from the Wal-Mart Corporation. Here is the story told by Holly Hospel, president of Ahh Hah!—Discovery Tools, a data mining company (www.AhhHah.com) in Indianapolis.

Wal-Mart, the world's largest retailer—with $165 billion in sales and 4,465 stores worldwide—began outstripping the competition, like Kmart, with intelligent use of data mining. The company was able to send electronic point-of-sale data from the checkout counter straight to headquarters. Then, data analysts could quickly determine if items should be replenished or if seasonal or emotional buying trends needed to be acted upon quickly. The company used the system to determine what items should be stocked, the quantity, the optimal location, and to facilitate sales analysis to determine the "right" price for a given product.

According to Randy Mott, Wal-Mart's chief information officer (CIO), "every cost, every line item, is carefully analyzed, enabling better merchandising decisions to be made on a daily basis. Customer buying trends and merchandise volume are under 24-hour 'surveillance.'"

Some of the ways Wal-Mart managers found to exploit their findings are legendary. One such legend is the story, "diapers and beer." Wal-Mart discovered through data mining that the sales of diapers and beer were correlated on Friday nights. It determined that the correlation was based on working men who had been asked to pick up diapers on their way home from work. On Fridays, the men figured they deserved a six-pack of beer for their trouble; hence the connection between beer and diapers. By moving these two items closer together, Wal-Mart reportedly saw the sales of both items increase geometrically. The lesson was not lost on the rest of the *Fortune* 500.

It is clear from this example that data mining allowed Wal-Mart to achieve two important objectives simultaneously. The first, of course, was to provide its shoppers with killer customer care by anticipating their needs with non-intuitive product placement that was unexpectedly convenient. The other objective was to increase sales dramatically, not an uncommon result for companies that focus on killer customer care.

Looking Ahead

Using customer information effectively is one of the more exacting strategies this book addresses for achieving killer customer care. Speaking and writing clearly is one of the simplest. We will tackle that topic in Chapter 17.

SPEAK AND WRITE IN PLAIN ENGLISH

COMMUNICATE CLEARLY ◀

There are two ways you can use words. One helps you to be understood. The other helps you to not be understood. You'll get much closer to achieving killer customer care if you stick with the first approach and avoid the latter.

Unfortunately—and amazingly—clarity is not the option many businesses choose. For reasons that we'll examine in a moment, these businesses allow their communication with their customers to be confused or garbled or otherwise unintelligible. In doing so, they are frustrating their customers, squandering selling opportunities, and creating an enormous obstacle to ever achieving killer customer care.

Despite what you may have heard, communication is not a two-way street, at least not in a customer care environment. All of the responsibility for effective communication lies with you. Your message to your customer—in person, online, and on paper—must be clear and understandable.

The Special Demands of Communicating with Customers

Communicating with customers is unlike other forms of communication you might be accustomed to. In almost any other communication situation you can think of, if one party is unsure of what the other party is saying, she or he will probably ask for some clarification. Customers, by contrast, are often unwilling to admit that they don't understand something. Rather than ask for an explanation, these customers will simply leave and go elsewhere. When this happens to your salespeople, they might perceive it as sales resistance or a lack of interest, but it is often just confusion hiding behind a façade of indifference.

The same phenomenon can occur in every other nook and cranny of your company where your employees speak, or otherwise communicate, with your customers.

I don't mean to suggest that clear communication is an easy or simple feat to accomplish. Quite the opposite is true—which is precisely why this chapter is so important. In fact, an important impediment to business communication is the fact that most people believe they're far better at it than they really are. As a result, they never make the effort to find out what their shortcomings are and, therefore, never improve.

Clear communication is not an innate talent for most people. It is a learned skill, and an absolutely necessary one for companies serious about killer customer care. In a moment, we'll review some techniques you can use to make sure your company communicates clearly with your customers. First, though, let's take a look at some other factors that get in the way.

The Biggest Impediment to Effective Business Communication

By a wide margin, the single biggest barrier to effective business communication is the widespread use of industry or company jargon. Certain industries are worse than others (the computer industry comes to mind as a particularly egregious offender), but there are few industries that do not commit this particular communication sin regularly.

It's not difficult to see why the problem of jargon is so pervasive. Industries and companies develop their own jargon as a shortcut to communicate concepts that would otherwise require longer, more time-consuming descriptions. This convenience is underscored by the fact that most people spend more time talking with their coworkers about work-related matters than they do talking with customers. Those two factors make the convenience of jargon difficult to forego.

For example, if you worked in the computer industry, it would be time-consuming and tedious to repeatedly refer to a "wireless networking protocol based on the 802.11b standard." It's much easier to talk about "Wi-Fi." When you're talking to a coworker or another industry insider, it's just as accurate and communicative.

The problem comes when one of your employees engages in a conversation with a customer and forgets to leave the jargon behind. Usually, the customer is less familiar with the current jargon but is reluctant to say so. A common response to this uncomfortable situation is for the customer to simply leave as quickly as possible. Your employee might sense some disconnect but probably doesn't realize why.

Technical terms are not the only kinds of jargon that alienate customers. Often, a company will have its own special vocabulary to describe a common situation or occurrence. As is the case with technical jargon, the use of these verbal shortcuts is fine as long as they're confined to internal communications. Trying to communicate with customers while using the company-insider vocabulary, however, does not enhance an environment predicated on killer customer care.

Other Barriers to Clear Communication

In addition to jargon, there are three other common factors in the poor communication process between businesses and their customers:

1. Lawyers
2. Lack of precision
3. Lack of attention to readability and navigability

Lawyers

Let's be clear about two points. Lawyers are absolutely necessary and provide valuable, even indispensable, guidance about important issues every business owner and senior manager must confront. The legal department cannot be the last word in your company when it comes to matters of customer care.

Legal protection for your business and killer customer care are certainly not mutually exclusive, but they're not the same thing, either, and your legal department is only focused on one of those concepts.

Your legal department will provide you with its own perspective on various issues, just as your accounting department will. In the end, though, as an owner or senior manager, you must make your own decisions about these issues. You must take everyone's perspective into account and synthesize a resolution based on your own judgment about what's best for the company. Relative to the issue of customer communications, some of the judgments you'll often have to make are: How much fine print is too much?

And how much "legalese" can be replaced by plain English?

You can enhance your relationship with your customer (along with your credibility) by eliminating as much fine print as possible and making sure warranties, disclaimers, and other "legal stuff" are written in an accessible style.

Legal considerations are important, but customer care considerations should—at the very least—be given just as much weight when business documents, advertisements, warranties, and other written materials are created.

Lack of Precision

We all have a distinct tendency to hear what we want to hear. In this respect, communicating with customers is *not* different from communicating with anyone else.

As a result, it is important to be precise when there is even the slightest danger of misinterpretation. A number of words and phrases that seem to suggest a value are, in real-

Direct Costs

A scene from Woody Allen's classic movie, *Annie Hall*, illustrates how these types of words can have dramatically different meanings to different people. In the movie, Alvy Singer (Allen's character) is involved in a romantic relationship with Annie (played by Diane Keaton) that is turning contentious. To help resolve their issues, both characters turn to therapy. A split-screen technique allows the audience to see Alvy talking to his psychiatrist on one half of the screen, Annie talking to hers on the other half, and hear both sets of dialogue simultaneously:

Alvy's Psychiatrist: How often do you sleep together?

Annie's Psychiatrist: Do you have sex often?

Alvy: Hardly ever. Maybe three times a week.

Annie: Constantly! I'd say three times a week.

If your business is like most, chances are some of your employees are engaging in conversations with your customers that reflect a similar kind of disconnect in the way language is used. In Alvy and Annie's case, "three times a week" is the reality. "Hardly ever" and "Constantly" seem to convey meaning, but they're imprecise.

> *One of the best innovations to emerge from the Internet is the use of a format known as FAQs, or "Frequently Asked Questions." Although this resource is most commonly found on Web sites, many companies have incorporated the concept into their paper-based materials, as well, allowing customers quick access to the information they are most likely to be seeking in a simple, highly readable question-and-answer format.*

ity, vague and imprecise. Words and phrases like "a lot" and "soon" fall into this category.

Lack of Attention to Readability and Navigability

If imprecise terminology jeopardizes killer customer care when it comes to your spoken communication, then poor readability and navigability do the same thing for your written communication—both online and on paper. We've already seen the particular danger to readability posed by your legal department, but most readability lapses are much more insidious. They're not deliberate obfuscations, as legalese can be. Rather, they're the result of well-intentioned but poorly crafted materials. The readability of a written communication is affected by two major factors.

The quality of the writing is the primary contributor to readability. Is your brochure or annual report written clearly and in a straightforward style? Written communications with customers should consist primarily of simple, declarative sentences. Solid writing skills are not possessed by everyone. If you're not fortunate enough to have someone in your organization with these skills, don't hesitate to go outside your company and hire the services of a freelance writer. Unlike spoken communications, written communications (especially those on paper) can exist for a considerable amount of time. It's worth the investment to make sure they're of the highest quality and won't be an embarrassment to you a year or two down the road.

Readability is also affected by navigability, which is how easily customers can find what they are looking for in your communication. The concept of navigability certainly applies to paper-based communications such as directions, policy statements, invoices, and marketing brochures, but it's especially true of your company's Web site. What information is your customer most likely to be searching for? Information about returns? Driving directions to your store? A list of services your company provides? These bits of basic information should be readily available in an easy-to-find, easy-to-access style.

A Simple Technique for Improving Communication

The simplest way to monitor the quality of your customer communications is to test them on someone outside the company, preferably someone who is not familiar with your products or services or even your industry.

Sit down with your Aunt Edna and see how easily she can figure out how to order a product on your company's Web site. Show copies of your returns policy to your teenage daughter's friends and see if they can read them and then explain them back to you. Give your next-door neighbor one of your products for free, on the condition that he allow you to sit and watch him try to put it together based on the directions that are included. Have Uncle Henry go to your sales office "undercover," listen to a sales presentation, then summarize for you what he thinks he heard.

All of these exercises are free. While the results they produce are what statisticians would call "anecdotal," they will certainly give you a great deal of insight into how effective your existing communications are—and how likely it is that those communications contribute to your company's ability to generate killer customer care.

Looking Ahead

If you're successful in implementing even a portion of the strategies and practices we've reviewed so far, there's no question that you'll have improved your business's level of customer care significantly. But achieving killer customer care is a little like winning a sports championship. It is often easier to *get* there than to *stay* there. In the final section of this book, we'll explore specific techniques you can use to maintain your business's performance level. And in the next chapter, we'll start with a concept that you might find surprising: diversity.

SECTION IV

▲ ▲ ▲

KEEPING YOUR KILLER CUSTOMER CARE PROGRAM ON TRACK

THE IMPACT OF A DIVERSE WORKPLACE ON CUSTOMER CARE

WHY DIVERSITY IS IMPORTANT AND PROFITABLE

Don't Skip This Chapter!

The fight is remembered in boxing lore as "the Saint Valentine's Day Massacre." It took place on February 14, 1951, in Chicago Stadium between Sugar Ray Robinson, still regarded as the best pound-for-pound fighter of all time, and Jake LaMotta, who was immortalized years later in Martin Scorsese's screen classic, Raging Bull.

Every once in a while, film from this riveting fight turns up on television. Although it's almost impossible to take your eyes off the combatants, when you do look past the fight for a moment, it is startling and almost eerie to scan the ringside crowd. Every single spectator in the first four or five rows at ringside—the only part of the crowd visible on the film—is a middle-aged white male. Every one.

Why You Shouldn't Skip This Chapter

Admittedly, few chapters in few books come with an admonition like "Don't Skip This Chapter!" Certainly there are plenty of other important chapters in this book, maybe even ones that will provide a more immediate impact on your killer customer care program. So, why does this chapter get special treatment?

Because I know many readers might be tempted to pass it over and move on to the next chapter, thinking they know what this one is all about. Perhaps a good place to begin this discussion is to review what this chapter is *not* about.

- It is *not* a discussion of social policy.
- Its objective is *not* to allow you to feel self-congratulatory.
- It is *not* an apologia for affirmative action.
- It does *not* suggest using your business as a platform for social change.
- It is *not* designed to make anyone feel guilty.
- It does *not* have anything to do with being politically correct.

This chapter is solely about a mindset, a strategic approach that can be both productive and effective for your business. Nothing more. But nothing less, either. If you dismiss the concept of diversity out of hand as being "soft," then you're overlooking an important and powerful tool for sustaining your ability to deliver killer customer care in today's marketplace.

A Rapidly Changing Business Environment

The world in which you're doing business is a different one, indeed, from the world in which Robinson and LaMotta fought in 1951. That world, of course, existed more than 50 years ago, and it's no surprise that things would change in that long a time period.

But a stark reality of today's business environment is that it no longer takes a half century for dramatic change to occur. Change is talking place at a rate that is literally unprecedented in history. That's not hyperbole; it's a fact. The rate at which we're forced to assimilate change is almost incomprehensible.

The Elements of Change

The breathtaking pace of change in our world is easiest to see in the areas of technology, but that is not the only arena in which rapid change has occurred and is occurring.

The demographic composition of your markets is changing rapidly, too, with profound implications for your strategies to create an environment of killer customer care. The market you're serving looks very different than it did a few years ago. Unless your business is somehow insulated from the rest of the world, you're dealing with a market that continues to change in terms of:

- Age
- Racial composition
- Gender roles
- Ethnicity
- Religious and social values

These areas are just some of the more obvious ones in which your marketplace is changing, and this list is by no means comprehensive. Moreover, the interaction among all of these elements is complex and dynamic. Changes in one area bring about changes in another, often in ways that are difficult to anticipate or even understand.

Just as your marketplace looks different, it also thinks differently. It behaves differently and has an entirely differ-

In the 1992 presidential campaign, Al Gore, then a vice-presidential candidate, sometimes sounded as though he were trying too hard to be a visionary when he talked about the emerging "information superhighway."

It is almost astonishing to recall that the entire Internet phenomenon—breathtaking boom, devastating bust, inevitable consolidation, and ongoing retrenchment—has occurred in such a relatively short period of time.

EThical Change

Whether all of that change is good or bad is a value judgment that is beyond the scope of this book. As Bertrand Russell, the 20th-century mathematician and logician, noted, "Change is one thing, progress another. 'Change' is scientific, 'progress' is ethical; change is indubitable, whereas progress is a matter of controversy."

You may or may not be enthusiastic about some aspects of the change you see around you in our society, but it is beyond question that you must address the fact that the environment in which you do business is, indeed, changing. If your business is to survive, ignoring change is not an option. Or, as U.S. Army Chief of Staff Eric Shinseki put it, "If you don't like change, you're going to like irrelevance even less."

ent set of values and sensibilities than it did even a short time ago. If your business is going to be able to understand its market and its customers on an ongoing basis, then you'll need a way to keep your finger on the pulse of your market's changing values. Killer customer care is impossible to achieve if you don't understand the values of the customers you serve. A diverse work force is the single most effective tool at your disposal to make sure your business stays closely in touch with your market as it changes.

One Danger of a Nondiverse Environment

A story has floated around for years concerning the internal discussions that took place in the early 1960s at the ABC television network about whether to proceed with the concept for a new show called *Wide World of Sports*. The story may be apocryphal—by its very nature, it would be a difficult story to pin down—but whether it's true or not, it is instructive.

The highly innovative *Wide World of Sports* went on to become a tremendous success and one of the longest-running shows in the network's history. But when it was first envisioned, some network executives were not convinced there would be a market for a weekly Saturday afternoon show about sports. During one heated debate about the show's viability, a network executive who was opposed to the idea, exclaimed in exasperation, "No one will be home to watch a show like this. On Saturday afternoons, everyone is out at the polo matches!"

Of course, not everyone was out at the polo matches on Saturday afternoons. But all of this executive's pals were.

That's the danger of a non-diverse environment. When you're surrounded by people who look like you do and think like you do, you'll never hear the things you need to hear about what's going on outside of your insulated environment. An insulated environment can be comfortable, but it's a dreadful perspective for learning what you need to know if you want your business to be able to consistently deliver killer customer care.

Another Important Aspect of Diversity

If killer customer care is your objective, then obviously your business environment should make your customers feel welcome. In Chapter 7, we examined a number of ways your employees can make your customers feel welcome, but no technique will overcome a business environment that makes some customers feel uncomfortable as soon as they walk in the door.

Your business environment should make all of your customers feel welcome. And your business will be a much more inviting environment for *all* visitors if your staff is drawn from a diverse population.

Hot Topic

Occasionally, there *are* valid business considerations that justify an environment that is not diverse—at least in certain respects. Hot Topic is a chain of stores that maintains a laser-like focus on selling apparel and accessories to customers in their mid-teens through mid-20s.

If a middle-aged male wandered into a Hot Topic store, it wouldn't take long before he said to himself, "This place is probably not for me."

He'd be right, of course. On the company's Web site, visitors are asked, "What's your scene?" The available choices on the accompanying drop-down menu are "Club," "Gothic,"

"Lounge," "Punk," "Street," "Rockabilly," and "Indie." Our middle-aged friend would probably be uncertain as to how to respond. (It should be noted that employees at Hot Topic have always been unfailingly helpful and polite to this middle-aged writer.)

In a store like Hot Topic, a reasonable business case can be made for creating an environment where certain individuals feel out of place. But, as a rule, "This place is probably not for me" is *not* the reaction you want from visitors to your business. It is simply too difficult to get to killer customer care from that particular starting point.

Recruit and Then Listen

Although it's true that the sight of a diverse staff conveys a valuable message to customers, the real point of a diverse work force is not to provide window dressing. The important thing about a diverse staff is not how it makes your company *look*. The important thing about a diverse staff is how it makes your company *think*.

Diversity is a powerful tool for forging an environment that supports killer customer care, but building a nonhomogeneous group of employees is only the beginning. You will be missing a tremendous opportunity if you don't actively take advantage of your employees' insights concerning your business, its customers, and its marketplace.

As decisions are made about new products, new markets, marketing and advertising campaigns, and other strategic issues, make sure that the "inner circle" making those decisions reflects these same principles of inclusion.

Looking Ahead

Even a diverse work force needs to be skilled when it comes to handling customer interactions. One of the touchiest interactions of all is when an employee asks a customer, "Was everything OK?" and the answer that comes back is a resounding "No!" In Chapter 19, we'll look at some principles for achieving killer customer care, even in that challenging situation.

> *Follow this simple rule of thumb. Look around at your company's next important meeting. If you find only people who look like you, then you haven't created the best possible environment for strategic decision making.*

ASK—BUT ONLY IF YOU WANT TO KNOW

GIVE CUSTOMERS THE CHANCE TO TALK TO YOU ◀

I*n Chapters 23, 24, and 25, we're going to delve deeply into techniques that will allow you to evaluate how well your business performs globally when it comes to delivering killer customer care. But there is a quick, inexpensive, virtually foolproof method you can use to see how well your business has performed in a specific transaction with an individual customer. This method is brilliant in its simplicity, yet powerful in its results. In addition, this practice is appropriate for businesses of all different sizes, in all kinds of industries; it can be used for simple retail transactions or complex business-to-business deals.*

Here, in its entirely, is the surefire method for learning how well your business performed in a specific transaction with a specific customer: Ask.

That's it. That's the whole thing. Of course, a few techniques your employees can use will be a bit more effective than others. But the important thing is to simply ask: ask every customer after every transaction if the transaction was satisfactory.

The Key Characteristic of a Killer Customer Care Environment

At its heart, this is what killer customer care is all about. You want to make sure every customer is pleased with every transaction. There's value in using some of the more comprehensive evaluation tools we'll explore later on, but if you do nothing other than ask each customer if he or she was pleased and then follow through on the answer until it's positive, you'd be well on your way to a terrific result. Organizational measurements and evaluations can accelerate your progress toward killer customer care significantly, but your most effective efforts are the ones that focus on making your customers happy, one at a time.

There are three reasons for verifying the outcome of every transaction with every customer:

1. To ensure each customer's satisfaction

Consider the Implications of Not Asking

Perhaps you can recall a time when you were on the customer's side of the counter in a transaction that was marginally unsatisfactory. It wasn't terrible, certainly not bad enough to prompt you to make a complaint but, for one reason or another, it just wasn't quite right.

There you stood at the checkout counter. The clerk took your money, counted your change, handed it back to you, and then ... turned his attention to something else. How did you feel? You probably wanted to say something like "Hey! Wait a minute. We're not done here. You guys could have done much better than that."

But you didn't. The transgression wasn't quite large enough for you to be determined to make it an issue, you were in a bit of a hurry, and the clerk was obviously not interested in your opinion one way or another. You weren't furious, and you weren't even particularly angry. Maybe you were a bit—peeved? Whatever precise word or phrase describes your reaction, it certainly wasn't anything close to what you'd have felt if you'd received killer customer care.

2. To get the information you need to avoid future problems

3. To convey to the customer your sincere interest in the result

To Ensure Each Customer's Satisfaction

Your objective for your business is to provide killer customer care for your customers. You can only reach that objective one customer at a time. If every customer's outcome is satisfactory, then your business cannot help but achieve its objective.

The key strategy is to make sure you're asking each and every customer. The size of the transaction doesn't matter, nor does the perceived importance of the transaction. This validation needs to be part of every transaction, just as delivering the product or service or collecting the money is part of every transaction. If you make this a habit (and you'll learn more about how to do that in Chapter 23), then you won't have to worry about an oversight that allows even a mildly dissatisfied customer to walk out the door with unexpressed irritation.

To Get the Information You Need to Avoid Future Problems

A memorable line in Ian Fleming's classic James Bond novel, *Goldfinger*, reads, "Once is happenstance, twice is coincidence, three times is enemy action." The same standard applies to instances of customer dissatisfaction that your employees uncover. An isolated instance should be addressed and noted, but it might be nothing more than an aberration or the personal quirk of a particular customer. If the same irritant turns up a second time, then your antennae should be quivering and your attention should be focused on the possibility that action might be required. One more mention of the same problem and you should be ready to mobilize your organization to do whatever necessary to resolve the situation. An organization that's intent on killer customer care doesn't allow problems to fester.

The thing to remember is that you will uncover irritants much earlier if your employees are validating each and every customer's satisfaction during each and every interaction.

To Convey to the Customer Your Sincere Interest in the Result

Even if your organization is performing splendidly and there are no irritants to address, there's still an enormous value in having your employees validate every customer's satisfaction every time. Verifying that every customer is pleased is perhaps the most powerful statement you can make about your organization's commitment to providing killer customer care.

Your marketing and advertising might say that your company is intent on pleasing its customers, but so what? Everyone else's marketing and advertising say the same thing. The only way to communicate your company's unshakable commitment to killer customer care is to demonstrate it. Not in some abstract way ("… surveys show 98.6 percent of our customers …") but in a tangible way. For *every* customer and *every* transaction.

When and How to Do It

There is a point in each transaction when your initial set of responsibilities has been fulfilled. In a simple retail transaction, that point comes early, when your employee takes the customer's money and hands over the merchandise. In a more complex transaction, the initial fulfillment of your responsibilities will come later, perhaps when the product is delivered and installed, or when the first in a series of services has been performed.

Whenever that point comes, you or your employees should ask a validating question. The specific wording that's appropriate will vary from one business situation to another, but here are some questions that are common across a variety of business environments.

- How was everything today?
- Did you find everything you were looking for?
- Are you pleased so far with what we've done together?
- Is this what you expected?
- How did we do?

The employee closest to the transaction should usually be the one to ask the question. Sometimes in the case of a more complex transaction, it might be appropriate to have a manager make contact with the customer at the end of the business deal specifically for the purpose of verifying that the customer is happy with the result.

What if the Answer Is Negative?

Sometimes when a validating question is asked of a customer, the answer is distinctly negative. When that happens, it's not uncommon for an unprepared employee to get unnerved. Often, the employee naturally reacts as though something bad has happened. It is important that all of your employees realize that—from a business standpoint—a *negative* answer is really a *positive* result!

If the employee hadn't asked the question and the customer hadn't answered, then that customer would have been dissatisfied upon leaving your store or office, but you

*H*ere's an important point: whoever is doing the asking should convey a sincere interest in the answer. A counterproductive result (to put it mildly) can occur if the customer perceives that the question was asked in a perfunctory or condescending manner.

wouldn't have known it, nor would you have had an opportunity to do anything about it.

When a customer gives a negative response to a validating question, you have uncovered a problem, you have been given a chance to resolve it, and you will often create a better impression on the customer than if there hadn't been a problem in the first place. In other words, your employees should understand that a negative response is not an indictment of the employee or the company. It's an opportunity to provide genuine killer customer care in a way sure to be appreciated and valued by the customer.

Looking Ahead

There are more sophisticated ways of evaluating your business's customer care performance, but few are more effective than simply asking. Sometimes, irritations are uncovered and can usually be addressed quickly. Other times, genuine problems are uncovered. (In fact, sometimes a customer with a problem will not wait for someone to ask. He might even track you down and tell you about it in no uncertain terms!)

When one of your customers has a problem, how it's handled makes all the difference in the world. That's why Chapter 20 is devoted to the subject of handling customer complaints.

> *The very worst thing an employee can do with a negative response is to ignore it. Few methods of infuriating a customer are more reliable than ignoring a problem once it's been pointed out. The customer's response—whether stated explicitly or not—is invariably "If you weren't going to do anything about it, then why did you ask in the first place?!"*

TURN COMPLAINING CUSTOMERS INTO ENTHUSIASTIC ADVOCATES

THE ART OF TURNING CUSTOMERS AROUND

L*ike death and taxes, customer complaints are unavoidable. If you're in business, there is no getting around the fact that you will someday wind up on the wrong end of a conversation with a complaining customer.*

It will happen regardless of the quality of your products and services, the degree to which you've trained your employees, or the extent to which your organization embraces the principles and practices of killer customer care. Although those things can dramatically reduce the frequency with which you must deal with complaints, there is no foolproof way to avoid complaints altogether.

In some cases, a complaint will have absolutely *nothing* to do with your company or your products or your employees. It will simply reflect the fact that your customer is having a very bad day, and you just happen to be in the wrong place at the wrong time. As a result, you wind up on the receiving end of a tirade. Is this fair? Probably not, but it is an inevitable part of being in business and dealing with people. It's helpful if your employees understand that fact so the inevitable won't throw them off stride. If your employees understand and anticipate that this sort of storm will blow into your business from time to time, they'll be much more in control of their reaction when it does.

It is also important for your employees to understand that, no matter how vile the behavior of a customer making a baseless complaint might seem, empathy is more appropriate than indignation. It's certainly possible that your customer recently endured some kind of tragedy, perhaps the loss of a parent or spouse. Although such loss is a rare occurrence, there's just no way of knowing. Your employees' most effective reaction when confronted by a customer who seems irrationally upset is to not take it personally, be rigorously nonconfrontational, and proceed through the steps we explore in this chapter.

As you'll see, the basic method for dealing with a complaining customer is the same, regardless of the circumstances or validity of the complaint.

Let's Face It: Sometimes There's a Screw-Up

Although there are customers who make irrational complaints, most of the time, the truth of the matter will be that somehow, something got screwed up, and your customer wound up getting the short end of the stick. It might be the fault of the employee who dealt with the customer, it might be the fault of someone else at your company, or it might be the fault of a third-party contractor like a delivery company. Even a heartfelt commitment to killer customer care cannot always prevent mistakes from happening.

When dealing with your customer's complaint, it doesn't matter who's to blame because, from your customer's standpoint, it makes no difference. A customer might mistakenly perceive an attempt to allocate blame as an effort to avoid responsibility. Besides, there will be plenty of time for post-mortems later. What matters now is the unhappy customer who is voicing displeasure (or worse) to one of your employees. The important thing at this point is not to assign blame but to address the matter at hand as effectively and expeditiously as possible.

The Six Steps for Dealing with a Complaining Customer

The most effective approach for dealing with a complaining customer can be distilled into six simple steps that your employees can easily recall by the acronym DEHEAT. Besides providing an easy way to remember the six steps, the acronym also supplies a ready reminder that, when things start to get hot, the objective is to cool them down. The six steps of the DEHEAT process are:

1. **D** eal with the customer, not the problem
2. **E** xorcise your ego
3. **H** ear the customer out
4. **E** mpathize
5. **A** pologize
6. **T** roubleshoot

Deal with the Customer, Not the Problem

Success with a complaining customer is, as much as anything else, a question of how the encounter is approached. If you focus solely on the problem, you could be in for a long and frustrating conversation. As we examined above, it's entirely possible that the underlying reason for the complaint has nothing to do with your business. Similarly, it may be something over which you have no control. You can't always fix the problem, but you can *always* try to make the customer feel significant and appreciated.

If you approach an encounter with a complaining customer with the attitude that you've got to "fix the problem," then you're likely setting yourself up for failure. On the other hand, if you approach the situation with the attitude that you're going to focus on alleviating the customer's frustration, then a variety of satisfactory outcomes are possible.

Exorcise Your Ego

The biggest pitfall that most employees (and most managers, for that matter) face in dealing with a complaining customer is an almost irresistible urge to "be right." The employee contradicts a customer who is "wrong"; the customer digs in; the situation escalates needlessly and, sometimes, uncontrollably.

It doesn't matter who is right. And if an employee wins the argument but loses the customer, then that's not much of a victory, is it? It's certainly not killer customer care.

In Chapter 10, we referred to the technique of "playing a role" in encounters with customers. If ego is interfering with the successful resolution of a complaint situation, then role-playing can be an extremely effective technique for avoiding that insidious trap. If a customer starts yelling or

*N*otice that the terminology in this chapter refers to dealing with a "complaining customer," not a "customer complaint." That rhetorical construction is no accident. It suggests the mindset you need for success.

acting in an unreasonable manner, then—in your mind— remove yourself from the situation and pretend you're in a movie, playing the role of a thoroughly businesslike but completely empathetic customer care specialist. Use this technique just a few times, and you'll become habitually more focused on results than on being right.

Hear the Customer Out

This may be the most important of the six steps. Few things you can do are as infuriating or as dismissive as interrupting a customer while he or she is in the middle of a complaint. The fact that you think you know what they're going to say doesn't make it any less infuriating to the customer. Or any less dismissive. Or, for that matter, any less rude. None of those characteristics is going to result in killer customer care.

Always hear the customer out—from beginning to end—before interjecting an opinion or suggesting a response.

If you're not in the habit of hearing out a complaining customer, you might be astonished at the results that this technique produces all by itself. Often, by the time a complaining customer gets to the end of his story, he has dissipated his anger and feels better merely for having had an opportunity to vent.

Clarifications

The only exception to the rule of hearing a customer out completely before speaking is when you need to ask a clarifying question. However, make certain your question is not one that can be construed as somehow undermining the customer's position. Don't ask, for example, something like "But you didn't call until after the warranty had expired, right?" That will not be perceived as a clarifying question; it will be perceived as an accusation.

This technique by itself, consistently applied, will dramatically improve the results you achieve when dealing with complaining customers.

Empathize

"… sharing the feelings of another." This is an important distinction to understand. It is possible to empathize with someone without necessarily agreeing with that person.

Regardless of the merits of a customer's particular complaint, it is an unquestionable fact that something is causing that customer to feel bad. A highly effective technique in dealing with that customer is to simply acknowledge his or her feelings. The most straightforward approach is some variation of this statement, "I can certainly understand how you feel." You're validating the customer's feelings without getting into a confrontation (or even a discussion) of the merits of his position.

Apologize

This part of the DEHEAT process is a natural extension of empathy and does not require you to shoulder blame or to make any admissions that the folks in your legal department would discourage.

The simplest apology is this: "I'm sorry that happened."

This straightforward response to your customer's plight will almost always help defuse a problem situation. Say it willingly and sincerely. (If you're standing listening to a customer complain, whatever the merits of the underlying issue, there's probably no doubt you're sorry it happened!)

It is only after you've apologized that your customer will be ready to move on to more productive and positive conversation. It's pointless to get stuck in an unproductive quagmire. An apology is a key element of successfully achieving killer customer care with a complaining customer.

Troubleshoot

Now, you've heard your customer out, allowing him to vent his frustration. You've empathized with him and, as a result, have ratcheted the emotional level of the situation down considerably. You've also apologized, further diffusing the situation and putting the ball in his court for a reciprocal demonstration of reasonableness. Now—and only now—it is time to address whatever problem has precipitated the complaint.

The nature of your business will define the parameters within which you can work. A good place to start, however, is simply to *ask the customer what it would take to resolve the situation satisfactorily*. You'll be astonished at how often the customer would be perfectly happy with a resolution that is significantly less than you would have been willing to offer!

Moving Complaints Through the System

Situations will arise when the person hearing the complaint is not the best person to resolve the situation. In those instances, if it's at all possible, your employee should refer the complaint, not the complainer.

In other words, your customer should not have to repeat the story once it's been told. The very process that allowed your customer's anger to dissipate the first time around might very well cause it to reemerge the second time through.

Once an employee has heard your customer's complaint, that employee should—if at all possible—take responsibility for moving the complaint through your internal systems, if that employee cannot handle the situation personally.

Looking Ahead

The best approach to dealing with complaints is to empower your employees to do whatever is necessary to make things right. In fact, that concept is so powerful, it's the subject of our next chapter.

EMPOWER YOUR EMPLOYEES TO MAKE THINGS RIGHT

EVERY EMPLOYEE IS A CUSTOMER SERVICE REP

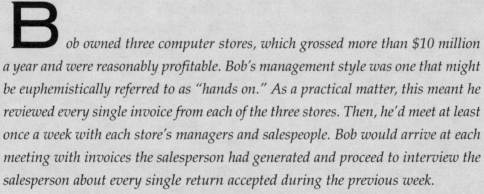

Bob owned three computer stores, which grossed more than $10 million a year and were reasonably profitable. Bob's management style was one that might be euphemistically referred to as "hands on." As a practical matter, this meant he reviewed every single invoice from each of the three stores. Then, he'd meet at least once a week with each store's managers and salespeople. Bob would arrive at each meeting with invoices the salesperson had generated and proceed to interview the salesperson about every single return accepted during the previous week.

It didn't take new salespeople long to realize that refusing to accommodate a customer's request for a return was significantly less stressful than dealing with Bob's weekly interrogation. As a result, the company's salespeople adopted a practice of citing a "company policy" against returns and forcing customers to talk directly to Bob if they pressed their case. Eventually, Bob's managerial style resulted in him regularly being more stressed out than he could handle, so he wound up selling his business for substantially less than it was worth.

The irony underlying this story is that Bob would usually admit the salespeople had acted properly in accepting returns, but not before making them offer many explanations and justifications for their actions. It was his refusal to give his employees the latitude to do their jobs that caused the breakdown of his business. His behavior resulted in employees who stopped exercising good judgment—or, for that matter, any judgment at all—and customers who were frustrated because they needed to expend so much effort to conduct what should have been a simple transaction.

Bob is an extreme example of a strategic and tactical weakness that is, unfortunately, all too common in businesses: a manager's or owner's reluctance to empower employees. Although the results of this shortcoming are seldom as pronounced as they were for Bob, killer customer care *always* suffers when well-trained, well-intentioned employees are hamstrung by suffocating management.

A Surprise Characteristic of Business's Elite

Thomas A. Stewart, writing in *Fortune Magazine*, made a noteworthy observation about traits common among the members of the magazine's "Most Admired Companies." This prestigious list is compiled from annual surveys of the country's top corporate executives. Companies such as Cisco Systems, Home Depot, the Container Store, and GE have, at one time or another, made it onto the elite list.

Stewart described his finding this way:

Each of these companies is clear about where it stands and where it is going. They're frank about their problems and their strengths. None have any doubt about vision, values, strategy, or mission. But they are clear about something else too. They have mission statements. They also have what might be called permission statements: a set of principles—some articulated, some tacit—that allows people to act on their own for the good of the company.

The Power of Empowerment

It's easy to dismiss the concept of empowering employees as some sort of new-age, feel-good substitute for solid management practice, but doing so is a mistake. Companies such as the ones mentioned in the sidebar are publicly traded, with a clear responsibility to shareholders. Judging from their results, those companies know a little something about management practice.

In general, the companies operate on the premise that, if you've done a creditable job of recruiting and training, your employees will want to do the right thing for the company and its customers. And, if that's the case, then the most effective approach management can take is to stay out of the way and not interfere.

Of course, management wants to do the right thing for the company and its customers, too. The disadvantage for managers is that they are seldom as close to the firing line as employees. Not only do employees have a better perspective on operational issues, but they also spend more time in direct contact with customers. Those front-line employees are ideally positioned to see and understand what needs to happen if the company is going to offer killer customer care.

Putting a Championship Team on the Field

Empowering employees does not mean management doesn't have a critical role to play. It does mean that management's role is considerably different than the one our friend, Bob, assumes it is. At its heart, the role of management is to facilitate the achievement of a company's objectives through the company's employees. This is accomplished through a four-part process:

1. Recruit the right team members
2. Define the goal
3. Provide the necessary tools
4. Establish the "sidelines"

Recruit the Right Team Members

Your ability to provide killer customer care begins when you undertake the effort and expense of finding and recruiting the best team of employees you possibly can. It is always easy to rationalize why recruiting has to sometimes take a low priority, but it is no exaggeration to say that you have no higher priority as a manager than to put the best possible team members in place. You can execute every other facet of your job flawlessly, but if you don't put a first-rate team together, your business will *never* be as successful as it could be.

If you have resisted the notion of empowering your employees, perhaps the underlying reason is that you didn't do as good a job as you should have in recruiting the best team. When you've established a first-rate team, empowering the individual team members becomes a self-evident next step.

Define the Goal

A critical function of management is to firmly establish the company's objectives in everyone's mind. These objectives include financial performance—and are often measured, at least partially, in financial terms—but they also include more abstract concepts like the company's values. As we saw in Chapter 2, it is necessary for you and your entire management team to evangelize your company's commitment to killer customer care. That evangelization process certainly falls under the category of defining the company's goals.

Your confidence in your employees' ability to make sound decisions about customer care issues will be enhanced significantly if you are certain they understand your goals and values thoroughly.

Provide the Necessary Tools

Merely defining a set of goals for the company is not nearly enough. Your next task as a manager is to provide your employees with the tools they need to get the company where you want it to go. The principle of empowering employees is meaningless if you don't provide them with the tools they need to succeed.

Provide them the training they need. Chapters 9 and 10 dealt extensively with the issue of training as it relates to your employees' ability to deliver killer customer care. Naturally, this training is above and beyond the job-specific training you provide. In general, it is not an exaggeration to say you cannot overtrain your employees. You can train them poorly, of course, but you can't *overtrain* them.

Provide them the information they need. If your employees are going to be able to deliver killer customer care, then they will need as much information as possible about your company, its products, and its services. They will also need information about the customer, which should be stored in a robust customer information system.

Establish the "Sidelines"

The final element of management responsibility is to help your employees understand what is and is not acceptable to you. An element of common sense comes into play here, but it is to everyone's advantage to explicitly provide your team with a general set of guidelines they can use in formulating decisions.

For example, at what point do profitability issues begin to outweigh customer care issues in a given transaction? It would be naïve to think that such a point doesn't exist, but the entire premise of this book is that the long-term health of your business is often achieved through tactics that are not the most immediately profitable ones at your disposal. Where, then, is the dividing line? If your employees have a firm grasp on the standards you use to answer that question, they will be in a better position to intelligently and effectively apply those standards without requiring your intervention.

Below are a few additional guidelines for empowering your employees.

Don't Nitpick

The fact that an employee did something differently than you would have does not mean he or she did it wrong. It's important for you to accommodate stylistic differences, as long as the employee's actions fall within the parameters you've established for customer care and profitability.

Don't Second-Guess Well-Intentioned Efforts

When you empower your employees, they will occasionally make mistakes. But, truth be told, if you were down

Mistakes Are Educational

There is a classic, decades-old story (possibly apocryphal) about Tom Watson, Sr., the father of the IBM Corporation. According to company legend, an IBM employee was summoned into Watson's office after making what proved to be a multimillion-dollar mistake (an even more significant sum of money then than now).

The employee assumed he was about to be fired and said as much to Watson. The canny executive's reply was "Nonsense. I just invested several million dollars in your education. It wouldn't make sense to fire you now."

there in the trenches being hands-on, you'd make some mistakes, too.

If your employees are ever going to be good decision-makers, they need to acquire experience doing it without you looking over their shoulders. Second-guessing them when things go wrong will only teach them to avoid making decisions in the future, precisely the *opposite* result of the one you're looking for.

Celebrate Stories about Customer Care Successes

A terrific way to teach your employees about correctly performing killer customer care is to tell them stories about other employees who did something right. Stories are

If You're Serious about This, Throw Away the Policy and Procedures Manual

A particular airline was once a chronically poor financial performer. It also had a long history of micromanagers who, over time, made it clear that employee empowerment was the last thing they wanted. (You may speculate for yourself about the connection between the airline's poor financial performance and the company's obsessive micromanagement.)

Over the years, the company's policies and procedures manual had evolved into a nine-inch-thick (!) tome that employees derisively referred to as the "Thou Shalt Not" book.

When the company was taken over by a management team committed to change, killer customer care, and employee empowerment, all of the employees at its corporate headquarters were summoned out to the parking lot, where the new CEO and the new president ceremonially put a copy of the "Thou Shalt Not" book into a trash can, doused it with gasoline, and set it on fire.

You will not be surprised to hear that the company's customer care performance and financial performance both improved dramatically.

It is true to the point of being clichéd to say that your company's employees can be your greatest asset. If your company is ever going to achieve that lofty level of performance that we call killer customer care, it is your employees who are going to get you there. But that can only happen if you empower them to take you there.

extraordinarily powerful vehicles for conveying values. (Isn't that how you taught your kids?)

Have a handful of stories tucked away in your back pocket, to pull out and share at an appropriate moment. Your employees will quickly and effortlessly learn about how to handle empowerment when they hear what their predecessors and colleagues did in the past.

Looking Ahead

Your employees may be empowered to provide killer customer care, but your relationship with your customer shouldn't end when the interaction has concluded. In the next chapter, you'll learn about an often overlooked ingredient of killer customer care: staying in touch after the sale.

STAY IN TOUCH AFTER THE SALE

SELLING DOESN'T STOP WITH THE TRANSACTION ◄

I t's dangerous to carry most analogies too far, so keep that caveat in mind as we explore one particular analogy to describe the relationship between your business (the pursuer) and your customer (the pursued). In many ways, the nature and progression of that relationship is like a promising relationship that has the potential to blossom into a long-term, mutually fulfilling connection.

The courtship begins with a tenuous flirtation. You learn about each other to see if there's a commonality of purpose and of values. After some period of courtship (which may or may not be lengthy), the relationship is finally consummated, that is, the sale is made. (A number of obvious jokes come to mind here. Keep in mind we've already admitted the analogy is not perfect!)

In most relationships, the prospect of a meaningful, long-term relationship can hinge entirely on what happens next. One possibility is continued attentiveness. In a courtship, that might mean flowers and phone calls the morning after. In business, it means follow-up contact after the sale. In fairy-tale cases, the relationship blossoms, and everyone lives happily ever after.

Another possibility is that the pursuer never calls again, leaving the once-pursued partner feeling unwanted, abandoned, and used. Such an ending is hard enough to understand when it happens between lovers, but it's genuinely unfathomable when it occurs between a businesses and its customer.

But before this analogy gets completely out of hand, let's turn our attention to the implications this scenario can have for your business.

Huge Opportunity for Differentiation

As we discussed in great detail at the beginning of this book, the whole point of killer customer care is to differentiate your business in a competitive market. Staying in touch with your customer after the sale is a tremendous opportunity to make your company stand out as you communicate that you are grateful for the business and would appreciate the opportunity to be of service again in the future.

The fact that so few businesses make the effort to do this consistently is particularly bewildering in light of the fact that today's technological environment makes staying in touch so easy and inexpensive. In fact, if you've followed some of the basic strategies outlined earlier in this book, then you're already most of the way toward creating a highly effective, highly efficient structure for maintaining contact with your customers after the sale.

Three Elements of Continuing Customer Communication

There are three basic elements of an ongoing communications structure between you and your customers:

1. A customer information system
2. A communication medium
3. A message

A Customer Information System

By now, it should be abundantly clear that a robust customer information system forms the absolutely critical foundation for almost every aspect of your killer customer care effort. It is the starting point for all your ongoing communications with your customers. After all, it is literally impossible to stay in touch with someone if you don't know their address, phone number, or e-mail address. On the other hand, possessing all three of those bits of information gives you a high degree of flexibility in choosing among various communication options. Moreover, you're able to tailor your communications to meet the requirements and preferences of the particular individual you're trying to contact.

Ongoing customer communications, then, is just one more reason to make your customer information system an absolute priority for everyone in your business. Data for every customer needs to be collected as early in the relationship as possible, then maintained regularly in order to ensure it's accurate and current.

A Communication Medium

There are three primary communication media from which you can choose. In crafting an ongoing communication strategy for your business, you can think of each one as a tool with specific characteristics that produce specific results. Which is the best way to stay in touch? That's like walking down the aisle of a Home Depot store and asking which tool is the best one. It all depends on your particular need at a particular time. Sometimes you need a hammer; sometimes you need a screwdriver. But your toolbox is incomplete without both.

The communications media that belong in your communications toolbox are:

Telephone. This tool is the most powerful one at your disposal. Its most effective use is for individualized communications in which the caller is prepared to address specific aspects of the customer's transaction. In particular, it is well suited for a follow-up call after a purchase or service event to make sure the customer is pleased with the result of that interaction. When this type of call is done properly, you will have the customer's transaction history or service information available at the outset of the call for reference. **Important point**: A phone call whose sole purpose is sales-related is not consistent with the principles of killer customer care under any circumstances. *Period*.

E-mail. Electronic mail is a mainstream communication medium that can be highly effective when used properly. Customers are sensitive about their e-mail inboxes, so this medium must be used with care. When a customer is asked to provide you with her e-mail address, the terms under which you will use it ought to be clearly outlined. If the e-mail information is provided for a specific purpose, then it should be used only for that purpose and for no other. However, there's nothing inherently wrong with the judicious use of e-mail for marketing purposes—as long as you have your customer's explicit permission to do so. The more circumspect you are in the use of e-mail, the more effective your e-mail communications will be. If e-mail from your business shows up in your customer's inbox every other day, then it will quickly lose its impact and your customer will ignore it.

Regular mail. Regular mail is fairly expensive, but it gives you the most latitude, partly because it is not regarded as being nearly as intrusive as the telephone or e-mail. Among its other advantages is the fact that it is far more persistent than other media. Although a phone call is completely ephemeral and e-mail is often deleted quickly, a mailing piece—particularly one that is creatively designed or otherwise intriguing—will often be set to the side of a customer's desk until she can get around to it.

A Message

Going back to our "morning after" analogy for just a moment, the basic message you want to convey after the sale is simple: thank you!

And, of course, as we saw in Chapter 19, it's certainly appropriate to embellish the message with a validating question or two to make certain the customer was pleased with the results of your interaction.

This is also a window of opportunity for certain strategically selected, highly targeted marketing efforts. A complementary product or service offered at an attractive price is not inappropriate, nor is it inconsistent with the principles of killer customer care.

When (and How) to Follow up for Maximum Effectiveness

When it comes to follow-up communications, a key variable that significantly impacts the effectiveness of your efforts is timeliness. Follow-up communication loses its effectiveness in proportion to the square of the elapsed time between the original interaction and the customer's receipt of the communication. OK, like so many other pseudoscientific formulas and statistics you read in business books, that formula is basically fabricated.

But you get the general idea. If you wait three weeks before sending a follow-up communication, it's lost almost all of its value. Killer customer care dictates that follow-up communications should go out *daily* in the immediate wake of the customer interactions that took place during that day.

> *A*ctual transactions are not the only interactions that merit some kind of follow-up. In many businesses, it would be appropriate to send a follow-up note to thank a customer for visiting your company, even if no actual business was transacted.

Principles for Designing Your Follow-up Communication Systems

Additional principles must be examined to help you design the most effective follow-up communication system for your business needs.

Use "boilerplate" communications when appropriate. If your business lends itself to the use of boilerplate communications, by all means use them. It is the immediacy, not the originality, of your communications with your customers that will engender a positive reaction. While boilerplate communications are sometimes criticized as being somewhat insincere, the more important reality is that your customers will appreciate your apparently insincere attentiveness more than they will appreciate your sincere neglect.

Accommodate your customer's communications preferences in your communication system. If a particular customer would prefer to not receive e-mail from you, then your system should reflect that. That doesn't mean the customer should be excluded from the information system altogether; it simply means customers should be able to choose which forms of communication they would prefer to receive from your company.

Include a reply mechanism in every communication you send to a customer. When you call a customer, you should give your toll-free phone number in case any questions occur to him or her after the call has concluded. If you send regular mail, it should also prominently feature a toll-free phone number as well as an e-mail address. And when you send e-mail, your customer should be able to reply directly from his or her e-mail program using the "Reply" button. E-mail from your company that requires a disclaimer that starts with "Do not reply to this e-mail …" is unacceptable.

The Concept of "Automated Tactics"

Often, your most effective follow-up communication will need to be structured to happen in multiple steps. For example, if you sell a new car to a customer, you might want to send a thank-you letter the following day, then call 10 days after the purchase to make sure everything about the car and the transaction has met the customer's expectations. In such cases, you'll want a communication system that offers "automated tactics."

In the example above, such a system would immediately produce a thank-you letter as the invoice for the transaction is generated. It would also automatically enter an event into the system's calendar that would trigger the follow-up phone call in 10 days.

This automation of multiple steps ensures that the all-important follow-up phone call doesn't fall through the cracks or get forgotten in the day-to-day press of business. And, as we discussed in the early chapters of this book, not allowing anything to fall through the cracks is virtually the definition of killer customer care.

Looking Ahead

Automated tactics programs are one way to make sure certain actions are taken by your business on behalf of your customer. Many others are discussed in other parts of the book. But how do you know whether everything is being done properly? You can create systems to guide your employees' behavior, but how can you monitor the spirit that surrounds your business's interactions with its customers? Take the approach pursued by Ronald Reagan when monitoring weapons agreements with the Soviet Union in the 1980s: "Trust, but verify." In Chapter 23, you'll learn how to "shop" your business to verify that it's achieving the level of customer care you want.

"SHOP" YOUR BUSINESS REGULARLY TO ENSURE QUALITY

DON'T TAKE YOUR QUALITY FOR GRANTED

Y our employees understand your company's commitment to killer customer care, and you've made certain senior management consistently provides leadership in this area by acting as role models. You've made sure all your employees are trained to respond to a variety of the most common situations they'll encounter. In fact, you've done everything you could think of to make certain your business is providing the highest, most consistent level of customer care possible.

As a result of all that, you have a great deal of confidence in how well your business is performing. You think you know everything you need to know about how well your business operates—but it's very unlikely that you do.

Seeing Your Business as Your Customer Does

Unless your company is a very small one and you're there personally all the time, it's virtually impossible for you to know exactly how well it's performing. That's because you don't see your business as your customer sees it. That's not your fault. It doesn't mean that you have some kind of inherent defect that prevents you from seeing things properly. Your problem is that unavoidable impediments standing in your way.

- It's difficult to see the overly familiar.
- You have an emotional investment in what you're seeing.
- Your perspective as a manager clouds your vision.

It's Difficult to See the Overly Familiar

If you've ever sold a home that you've lived in for a long time, you've probably experienced this phenomenon. Over the years, you had become so thoroughly familiar with your home that there were many features—both positive and negative—you simply stopped seeing. They became so much a part of the environment that they stopped registering on your consciousness. Eventually, it became impossible to see them even when you thought you were conducting an objective inspection of the premises.

It was only when the real estate agent did a first walk-through of the house that you began to see some things that were there all along but had faded from your conscious view. Even more startling was the assessment of the property that was performed by the home inspector before the closing.

In similar fashion, unless you're a new member of the company's senior management team, you've probably been hanging around your business too long to be able to

Authors often fall prey to the overly familiar phenomenon. It is common for an author to hand a publisher a manuscript in "pristine condition," only to have an eagle-eyed copy editor find hundreds of typos, misused words, and misspellings.

see it with fresh and objective eyes.

You Have an Emotional Investment in What You're Seeing

Garrison Keillor's fame on the radio was built substantially on his folksy tales about the fictitious community of Lake Wobegon, where "the women are all strong, the men are all handsome, and the children are all above average." It's not difficult to see humor in the fact that all the good people of Lake Wobegon think their children are above average. The joke, of course, is that in any given group, half must be below average *by definition*. But it's not so easy to see this dynamic at work when we're in the middle of it.

As we noted in Chapter 1, it is almost impossible to find a business owner or senior manager who does not fervently believe his or her business does a terrific job taking care of its customers. (It's probably true that all businesses in Lake Wobegon are above average, too.) This is not nec-

The Edward Clark Haskell Effect

Older readers (and younger readers who regularly watch Nick at Night) will instantly recognize Eddie Haskell as the smarmy friend of Wally Cleaver on the sitcom *Leave It to Beaver*. One Web site devoted to the television classic said of Eddie, "Eddie's two trademarks are his unctuous politeness to adults and his weasly, sharp-tongued meanness to everybody else." In other words, Eddie behaved quite differently when authority figures were around.

You shouldn't be surprised if your employees sometimes behave like Eddie Haskell. This is not meant as a slight; it's just a reflection of a natural tendency that we all have to be on our best behavior when we know someone is watching—particularly when that someone is the boss.

Unfortunately, your business's reputation for customer care will not be defined by your employees' best behavior. It will more likely be defined by their worst behavior or, at least, their average behavior.

essarily a bad thing. After all, an almost evangelical faith in your business is a distinct asset when you're out in the marketplace, competing for every customer and every sale. On the other hand, it can also be something of a disadvantage when it comes time to dispassionately assess your business's performance and identify its faults.

Your Perspective as a Manager Clouds Your Vision

If a particular system or procedure is not meeting your customers' needs, it might be difficult for you to see because that system is meeting *your* needs so well! There is an irresistible tendency to design our work experience as much as we possibly can to meet our own needs. It's extremely difficult to see the customers' side of a problem when a system or procedure is working well for us as managers.

Even "hands-on" managers do not always understand what it's like to be a customer of their own businesses. It's only natural that your own perspective gets in the way.

Shopping Your Business

The best way to get around all of these impediments is to periodically enlist the aid of an objective third party to act as a customer and to report his or her findings back to you. This paid "shopper" is able to do several important things that you, as a manager, cannot. He or she can

- Look at your business environment from a fresh, unbiased perspective
- Assess your business anonymously and "invisibly"
- Benchmark areas of performance that can be measured
- Provide unbiased qualitative evaluations of employee performance

Look at Your Business Environment from a Fresh, Unbiased Perspective

If you live in an *Architectural Digest*-quality home, you still reach a point where it no longer impresses you when you walk in the door every evening. You become complacent about its beauty. Similarly, if you live in a dump, you eventually become inured to its unsightliness.

A shopper will see your business without the baggage of history, either good or bad. He or she will be able to tell you what it's like to walk in the front entrance in a way that's difficult or impossible for you to see for yourself.

Assess Your Business Anonymously and "Invisibly"

When you're the person signing the paychecks (literally or figuratively), your employees are keenly aware of your presence and, whether your realize it or not, your presence causes them to behave differently than they would if you weren't there. As a result, you never get the opportunity to see how they behave when you're not there. There's nothing sinister about this. It's human nature. Your challenge as a manager, though, is to ensure that the behavior you never get to see is still up to killer customer care standards.

A shopper gets to see those behaviors you will never see. And he or she sees them "up close and personal," as the ostensible customer.

Benchmark Areas of Performance That Can Be Measured

There are aspects of your employees' interactions with customers that can be quantified. For example, how long does it take before employees greet a new customer arriving at your store? Or how long does it take before a party of four is seated at your restaurant? Or does the receptionist offer a cup of coffee to the visitor waiting to see a salesperson? All of these questions can be answered with a yes, a no, or a number.

Provide Unbiased Qualitative Evaluations of Employee Performance

In addition to quantitative measures, a shopper can collect impressions that are not strictly measurable because they are more subjective, but they are nevertheless significant. An experienced shopper can tell you if the interaction "feels" right—whether the employee was engaged in the conversation, whether he or she was distracted or preoccupied during the interaction, whether the employee seemed to care if the transaction went well or not.

As is the case with quantitative measures, a single impression is not necessarily going to provide you with a basis for analysis or decision-making. Anyone can have an occasional bad day—even a shopper. But multiple visits by shoppers over time will provide you with a textured insight into what it's like to do business with your company.

Using Shoppers Properly

If shopping your business is to be an effective tool, then it's important you approach it properly. The objective of shopping your business is not to catch your employees doing something wrong or to be punitive. If your employees don't perform well when they are shopped, your default assumption as a manager ought to be that you need to do a better job training. When your employees perform poorly, it is not even necessarily useful to apprise them of the fact that they were shopped at a particular time and underperformed. A more effective approach can be to simply

> *A* single measurement is not what statisticians call "statistically significant," but the cumulative results of a number of measurements taken over time tell an important story. Your shoppers can collect numbers that will provide objective measurements of specific behaviors you've identified as significant in providing killer customer care in your business.

step up your training in the areas that need more work.

Conversely, one of the most effective uses of this tool is to catch your employees doing something right. If your employees do a terrific job, then it's a very good idea to let them know that the business was shopped at a particular time and that they excelled. It's even more effective if you can do this immediately following the shop, and it's more effective, still, if you couple your plaudits with a more tangible show of appreciation, e.g., a reward or bonus. It's not necessary that this be something big in order to make a big impact. The degree of impact is determined by the immediacy and by your enthusiasm for the good work they did.

Some Additional Rules for Shopping Your Business Effectively

This technique needs to be a process not an event. Shopping your business once or twice has marginal value, if any. It is only by doing so regularly over a long period of time that you can gather the information you need to instill a consistent environment of killer customer care.

This technique can be used by businesses of any size. Shopping is not something only for large companies that can afford a service. Of course, if you have multiple locations or a large sales volume, the investment in a professional service will certainly pay off. On the other hand, if you're a small company, don't think that this process is out of your reach. Enlist the aid of a friend or neighbor—someone who isn't known to your employees—to accomplish many of the same results.

Don't be secretive with your employees about hiring shoppers. Let them know that this is a tool that you use to enhance the customer care performance of the business.

Assure them you're not trying to catch them doing something wrong. If your employees discover you're shopping the business and you haven't told them to expect it, you will unnecessarily create distrust between you and them.

Looking Ahead

"You can't improve something unless you can measure it," according to a manager's maxim, so that's why it's important to measure employee behaviors that impact killer customer care. In addition to quantifying behaviors, however, it's also possible to quantify the degree to which your customers are pleased with your business. Measuring customer satisfaction is the subject of our next chapter.

MEASURE CUSTOMER SATISFACTION

SYSTEMATICALLY EXPLORE WHAT MAKES THEM HAPPY ◀

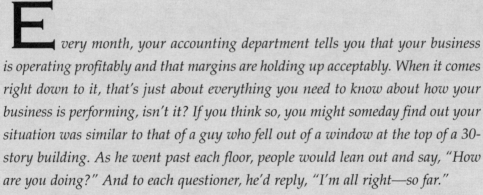

Every month, your accounting department tells you that your business is operating profitably and that margins are holding up acceptably. When it comes right down to it, that's just about everything you need to know about how your business is performing, isn't it? If you think so, you might someday find out your situation was similar to that of a guy who fell out of a window at the top of a 30-story building. As he went past each floor, people would lean out and say, "How are you doing?" And to each questioner, he'd reply, "I'm all right—so far."

Profitability tells some of the story about how well your business is doing, but it certainly doesn't tell the whole story. Some problems don't manifest themselves on your income statement until it's too late to address them easily. By the time they take a bite out of your profits, you're deeper in a hole than you had ever suspected, and digging out, if it's even possible, will be tough.

How can you avoid these traps? Occasionally, you can't. Companies that manufactured vinyl records at the end of the 1970s were about to be swamped by a tidal wave washing over the music business. Whether they realized it or not, their world was on the verge of major change, and there was no way to avoid it.

Most of the time, though, the story is less dramatic and far more amenable to preventative action.

Leading Indicators

An effective strategy for finding a problem in your business before it wreaks havoc involves the use of leading indicators. For example, the government uses a series of statistics called "leading economic indicators." These are measurements that, over time, have been shown to presage larger changes in the economy. When the indicators are going up, a good economy is likely to follow shortly.

When it comes to your business, your customer care performance is a leading indicator of how you will likely perform in the future, especially when the economy takes a turn for the worse. Businesses that provide killer customer care are simply better positioned to weather a wide variety of economic conditions than similar businesses that engender less customer loyalty.

So, How Do You Know?

As we've already seen, your own impressions of your business's customer care performance are not reliable for a variety of reasons. The feedback you get from shopping your business is helpful but it isn't adequate. The people who best know whether or not you are providing killer customer care are your customers.

*E*specially in a good economy, it's possible for serious problems to remain hidden, camouflaged by positive financial performance. When the economy shifts, though, these problems can manifest themselves quickly and dramatically. The problems can be like termites, silently and invisibly compromising the foundation of your business. There are only two ways to know the pests are there. The first is to wait for your structure to collapse. That's not a great approach for either your house or your business. The alternative is to look for signs of problems before the holes appear in your foundation.

If you really want to know how well your business is doing, you need to ask your customers. And, once you ask them, you'll want to track the results in a format that can serve as a management tool in the same way the financial reports from your accounting department serve as management tools.

This means you need information that's *quantified*. You'll get quantifiable information by taking measurements of your business's customer care performance over time and comparing periodic results—from month to month or year to year—just like you do with financial information.

What Should You Measure?

Measuring financial performance is straightforward. Over time, standards have evolved concerning what to measure and how to measure it. These standards are referred to as Generally Accepted Accounting Principles (GAAP). They're indispensable for the role they play in conferring objective meaning to financial data. As a matter of convenience, they are helpful because every business knows what to measure and how the measurement is supposed to be taken.

Unfortunately, no such standard exists when it comes to customer care performance. There is no widely accepted methodology for measuring the degree to which your business achieves killer customer care. The serious development of such standards would require an enormous undertaking. Until it happens, here are some questions you can pose to your customers about your business's customer care performance. These are, of necessity, generic questions you'll need to modify for your own situation.

These questions are divided into three categories. The first category is designed for a numerical response on a scale of one (worst) to five (best). The second category is for yes or no responses. The third category elicits demographic information. When you pose these questions to customers, it is not strictly necessary that you group them together in this way, but it tends to make things easier for your customer to follow if you do.

On a Scale of One (Worst) to Five (Best)

- Overall, how would you categorize your last transaction with The Acme Company?
- How helpful were our employees to you as you considered your decision?
- How knowledgeable were Acme's employees about the products you were considering?
- How interested were Acme's employees in your specific needs and requirements?
- How satisfied were you with the range of options you were presented?
- If you were in the market for another widget, how likely is it that you would return to The Acme Company?
- How likely would you be to recommend The Acme Company to a friend or colleague who was in the market for a widget?

Yes or No

- Were you greeted promptly when you arrived at The Acme Company location?
- Did the sales associate take time to find out what you needed?
- Did the sales associate explain the warranty policy to you?
- Did the sales associate tell you about the Customer Service Hotline for any questions you might have?

The questions you pose to your customers needn't be static. Over time, as you change your customer care focus from one area to another, you will want to modify your list of questions to reflect changing priorities. That makes perfect sense. But don't fall into the trap of thinking that you don't need to monitor a specific area—at least from time to time—after you've achieved acceptable performance in that area of customer care.

- Were you able to locate everything you needed?
- Were you able to quickly find a sales associate or other team member when you needed one?

Demographic

- Is this the first time you have shopped/purchased from this location?
- If yes, where have you typically shopped/purchased in the past?
- If not, how often have you shopped/purchased here in the previous six months?

How to Measure Effectively

If you're a large business, you should consider enlisting the services of a company that specializes in market research. Such a company can offer guidance in the best ways to design your questions, collect information from your customers, and interpret the information once it's been collected.

If you're not a large business, however, don't be reluctant to collect the information yourself. It will provide you with the valuable insight you're looking for to ensure that your killer customer care program is on track. You need only to follow a few simple guidelines, which we'll discuss here.

Select respondents so your sample is representative of your customer base. Let's say you have two stores that are each open from 10 A.M. to 9 P.M. If you chose to only survey customers from one store and then did so just once at 10:30 A.M., you could very well wind up with a sample that is unrepresentative of your entire customer base in several respects. Your customers in the second store might, for some reason, be different from the customers in the first. Also, if you only survey customers in the morning, you're likely to get a sample that underrepresents your customers who have conventional nine-to-five jobs.

For your information to be valid, it must represent a large-enough sample size. Ideally, you'd want to get feedback from every customer of your business. Usually, that's not possible, so you wind up surveying a subset of your customers. Make sure that the subset is large enough to avoid anomalies. To offer an extreme example of this problem, if you surveyed just one person, that person might come back with completely outlandish replies. Your odds of getting useful feedback improve when you ask a second person, get even better when you ask a third, and so on. If you're doing this yourself, you don't need to worry about getting a sample that is "statistically significant." You just need to make sure you're questioning enough people to avoid being pointed in a demonstrably wrong direction.

Use multiple means of collecting information. You have customers who wouldn't be comfortable answering questions in person but who wouldn't mind filling out a survey via e-mail. Other customers would prefer to fill out a form and return it in a postage-paid mailer. Still other customers would be most comfortable answering questions after the sale on the phone. It may not be possible to use all of these methods all of the time, but make sure you're not inadvertently excluding a segment of your customers by relying too heavily on one or two data collection methods.

How to Ask

Asking for customer feedback is a straightforward task. Most customers understand the process, so it doesn't require a great deal of explanation. It is worthwhile, though, to emphasize that your objective is not to sell any-

*G*enerally, you cannot survey each and every one of your customers, but there are exceptions to the rule, of course. When you sell large-ticket items, such as cars, it makes perfect sense to incorporate customer care questions into routine follow-up calls that are made to every single customer. Add the questions to your efforts for following up the sale along the guidelines we discussed in Chapter 22.

thing to the respondents but instead you simply want their insight and advice. And, if possible, it doesn't hurt to offer a small incentive for their participation.

Here is an actual letter (slightly modified) that illustrates how one airline solicits participation in an online survey:

Dear Customer,

You have been selected to participate in an important new satisfaction tracking study for Acme Air.

At Acme Air, we use several methods to measure our customers' satisfaction. You may have encountered an interviewer in the airport administering surveys, for instance. While these initiatives are critical for us to understand how we are performing on a given day, we would like to better track our frequent customers' overall satisfaction independent of a particular day's experience.

To that end, we will be sending an overall satisfaction survey to you every month. The questions in this survey will be similar to our other satisfaction surveys in that they will cover every aspect of the travel experience from reservations to baggage claim, as well as overall impressions. However, this survey will be different in that we will ask you your overall satisfaction with each attribute, rather than your satisfaction with a specific experience.

We plan to track these survey results over the long term, so we would greatly appreciate your participation every time the survey is sent (as your schedule allows).

This survey will take approximately ten minutes to complete. You will be awarded 250 bonus miles for completing the survey. This incentive will be offered each time the survey is sent to you in the future. Because the survey will be sent monthly, it will only be open for one week each time.

If you no longer wish to receive future mailings of this type, or wish to change your e-mail address or password, go to http://www.acmeairadvisorypanel.com, go to the "My Account" page and click on "Log in."

Thank you in advance for your participation in this study.

Sincerely,

Richard Blaine
Director, VP, Acme Air Customer Care

Not bad. The airline explains the nature and purpose of the survey thoroughly, provides an appropriate incentive for the customers' time, and offers an opt-out mechanism for customers who don't want to participate.

Using the Information You Accumulate

Contrary to popular wisdom, knowledge is *not* power. Rather, knowledge is only potential power. It only becomes powerful when you use it. The information you collect when you survey your customers about your business's customer care performance is not going to help that performance until you put it into the hands of the people who can make a difference.

The information you collect should be widely distributed among all of your company's employees, at least in summary form. And all of your managers should have the opportunity and ability to drill down into the data as far as they'd like.

Use this information as a management tool and as a motivational tool. Let your employees see what they're doing well and what areas still need improvement. Set quantifiable killer customer care goals and then let your employees loose to achieve them.

Qualitative and Quantitative Measures

Surveys like the ones we've discussed in this chapter are designed to uncover quantitative information about how your company is performing. As we saw in Chapter 23, qualitative or "anecdotal" feedback also has a role to play in supporting your killer customer care efforts.

When designing your surveys to elicit quantitative feedback, you can certainly give your responding customers the opportunity to expand upon their answers if they choose to do so. That type of qualitative feedback mixed with the quantitative replies can often be extremely eye-opening.

Don't indulge any temptation to keep this information under wraps. If the news is bad, then use it to underscore your commitment to making it better. And if it's good, then use it to reinforce the behaviors that made it so. Keeping this information from your employees would be like a football coach trying to keep the score from his players. It doesn't make sense.

Looking Ahead

In addition to the measurements we discussed in this chapter, you can get another kind of feedback from your customers that is more detailed, more nuanced, and can provide you with significantly more insight into how your business can achieve and maintain an environment of killer customer care. In Chapter 25, we're going to examine the use of focus groups, a specialized management tool designed to allow you to get deep inside the minds of your customers.

USE FOCUS GROUPS TO HONE YOUR INSIGHT

A WAY TO RESEARCH WHAT YOUR CUSTOMERS CARE ABOUT ◄

I magine this. In your quest to take your business to a new and unprecedented level of killer customer care, you have managed to identify and recruit an elite group of advisors. This select task force is made up of individuals with an extraordinary insight for the likes and dislikes of your very best customers.

This group acts as a brain trust for you and your colleagues in upper management, giving you detailed feedback on the effectiveness of your existing customer care efforts as well as a keen perspective on how well future efforts are likely to be received. As an added bonus, this remarkable group will occasionally be able to suggest some unique tactics for achieving killer customer care that have never occurred to you or any of your managers. Used strategically, the advice you get from this group will provide you with a distinct edge in your marketplace and keep you comfortably ahead of your competitors in the battle for customer loyalty.

If this sounds like the kind of wishful thinking and fantasy you usually indulge in only with your bankers and investors, then you're going to find the power and simplicity of customer focus groups to be quite a revelation.

The Most Basic Idea in the World

A focus group can tell you how well your current customer care efforts are being received by your customers. Are your efforts generally on track? Are you attempting to do the right things but falling short when it comes to execution? Or are your efforts conceptually off track so that even outstanding execution will not cause them to be well received?

The concept of the customer focus group is extremely simple. The idea in its most basic form is to gather together a group of customers (or potential customers) and listen to what they have to say about your business and its marketplace. That's it. There's nothing very complex or remarkable about it. Like so many other tools for achieving killer customer care, the real issue is not the sophistication of the tool. It is primarily your willingness to use it.

There are some guidelines for using this tool effectively. These guidelines are simple to master and leave plenty of room for you to adapt the concept of customer focus groups to meet your business's specific situation.

- Talk to the right group of customers.
- Make it easy for them to be thorough and candid.
- Keep the conversation on track.
- Don't be too intrusive.
- Keep an open mind about what you hear.
- Don't interpret your results through the prism of your own prejudices.

Talk to the Right Group of Customers

It doesn't make sense to expend a great deal of time and effort to get to a result that isn't what you really want. If you're going to the trouble of conducting a focus group, then you should make sure your effort is going to do more for your business than allow you to pursue market segments that are neither fun nor profitable. That's why your first and, perhaps, most important task in conducting a focus group is to make sure you're talking to individuals who represent the market you *want* to do business with, not necessarily the market you do business with today.

A productive focus group is composed of two types of customers. Any given focus group session may include members from either group or from both groups.

The first group you'll want to include represents your best existing customers. Which customers consistently generate the highest volume of sales dollars, month after month? Which consistently purchase your highest-margin products and services? Which have been the most loyal over the years? These are the customers whose insights will be useful in guiding your business to a higher level of profitability.

How do you identify these customers? By analyzing the data in your customer information system, of course. In addition to all of the other reasons we've discussed throughout this book for maintaining an accurate, up-to-date customer information, targeting customers who meet a desired profile will make your customer focus group significantly more effective than it would have been otherwise.

The second group you'll want to include is the type of customer you'd like to do business with but have not been able to attract. Perhaps Vulcans seem like an attractive segment of the market to you, but you've been doing business primarily with Klingons. Your problem, of course, is that inviting only Klingons who are your existing customers to be focus group members is not going to generate information about how to attract Vulcans.

Don't hesitate to go outside your existing customer base to recruit the group members you need. Of course,

> *It is not being negative to acknowledge that every business has customers who are not profitable and are certainly not fun. Try not to include any such customers in your focus groups. These customers have nothing valuable to tell you because the last thing you want to do is attract more customers like them.*

these noncustomer group members will not be able to provide much insight into your existing customer care efforts, but if your objective for a particular focus group is to explore possibilities for potential new programs or products, then a focus group that includes noncustomer members from your target market is a useful approach.

Make It Easy for Them to Be Thorough and Candid

If the customer surveys we discussed in Chapter 24 are designed to be wide, then focus groups are designed to be deep. Their purpose is not to provide you with the broadest possible view but, rather, to give you a more textured look at the relative success of your company's push toward killer customer care. It's important, then, to design your customer focus group so it's as conducive as possible to your goal.

Keep the size of the group manageable. If you've selected your group members carefully, you should have somewhere between five and 10 members. Having too few group members provides too little opportunity for interaction and discussion. It also increases the possibility that a particularly vocal group member might dominate the proceedings. Having too many group members means not everyone will have an opportunity to speak up.

Allow enough time to cover everything you want to cover. A highly effective tactic for accomplishing this is to conduct your focus group over dinner. This gives your attendees a tangible reason to contribute their time. A dinner meeting also tends to create a social atmosphere that makes group members more amenable to uninhibited conversation. And, if you're not averse to a bit of benign manipulation, it also confers on your attendees a sense of obligation to stay until the end.

Keep the Conversation on Track

If your focus group is going well, your attendees will be relaxed and responsive. That's positive, but it could also lead group members to get *too* relaxed and responsive. The most successful focus groups are conducted within fairly well-defined parameters. Your job as host is to make sure the conversation stays within those parameters. If your attendees get sidetracked onto a topic that does not support the meeting's objectives, gently but firmly put things back on track. (Think about Tim Russert questioning an evasive politician on *Meet the Press,* and you'll have a good idea of how to proceed!)

Don't Be Too Intrusive

Don't forget that your main function at a focus group is to listen, not interject your opinions or rationalizations. Although you need to be firm when it comes to keeping the proceedings on track, you need to remember that this is your customers' forum, not yours.

It's easy to sit back and listen when everyone is being complimentary about your business. But the first time someone rips apart what you thought was a terrific effort at killer customer care, you will find the temptation to jump in with a justification almost irresistible.

However much you feel compelled to explain yourself, any attempt to do so will put an abrupt end to any value your focus group might have been creating. Your customers didn't give up their valuable time to argue with you or to feel as though they have to validate their opinions. As soon as they feel that way, they will stop offering candid input. If there's something egregious that absolutely needs to be addressed, wait until the end of the meeting. Then, if

Keep in mind that when you schedule your focus group meeting can affect participation. If the customers you want to talk to are businesspeople, you're better off scheduling something in the evening rather than during the day. If your customers have to choose between completing your focus group and getting back to work, your event is going to wind up losing out every time.

it's feasible, address it privately with the individual who made the remark.

Keep an Open Mind about What You Hear

Over the course of an evening, you're likely to hear some fairly wacky ideas. Your customers have little or no concept of the economics of your industry or the logistical reasons why you think things should be done in a particular way. As a result of that ignorance, they'll make suggestions that you know are completely out of the question.

Or, at least, you *think* you know they are completely out of the question.

Most of the time, your initial impression—"That's crazy!"—might be absolutely correct. Every once in a while, though, you'll come across an idea that is a genuine breakthrough, something so "outside the box" that it never could have occurred to anyone but an outsider.

Don't Interpret Your Results Through the Prism of Your Own Prejudices

Consultants refer to this concept as a willingness to break through your "limiting paradigms." Whether you call them paradigms or prejudices, you have a set of beliefs that define how you interpret information. Although difficult to do, it is important for you to set these beliefs aside when considering what your customers have to tell you.

For example, you might hear a customer say she needs more help when trying to select from among your service offerings. If, before your focus group took place, you'd had an inclination to increase the number of service advisors your business provides over the phone, you might be inclined to interpret her comment as one that reinforces your belief. In reality, though, her concerns might be better

*D*on't dismiss out of hand anything you hear in your customer focus groups, no matter how unworkable it seems at first. Mull it over. Sleep on it. Poke it around a little bit. Sift through your customers' ideas and suggestions as though you were panning for gold. You might go through an awful lot of dirt, but it will be more than worth your time if, at the end of the process, you uncover a nugget or two.

The Strengths and Limitations of Focus Groups

In the last chapter, we noted that customer surveys can provide quantitative and qualitative data. Customer focus groups, by contrast, provide only qualitative information. Don't expect the information you get in a focus group to paint a broad picture of your customer base or one that reflects the outlook of all your customers.

Instead, think of your focus group as a magnified view of one small piece of a larger picture. It's valuable to you because it provides the shading and granularity that you might not notice when you look at the big picture.

Information you glean from customer surveys lends itself to dispassionate, left-brain analysis. What you learn from a customer focus group, on the other hand, is likely to elicit a more abstract, right-brained type of response. Neither approach to killer customer care is inherently superior to the other. Rather, they are complementary. You and your management team will make better decisions when you're reviewing both types of information regularly

addressed through the use of an online "wizard" that guides her through a series of questions and then makes a recommendation based on her answers. Such a solution could not only provide better service but also lower your costs.

Killer customer care can take many forms. Don't overlook any of them because your built-in assumptions act as blinders.

Guidelines for Making Your Focus Group Work

As you might expect, conducting a focus group can be as much art as it is science. Still, following these few guidelines will help make your focus group as productive as possible.

- *Prepare a basic agenda.* As you convene your group, you should have questions prepared to ask during the course of the meeting. The best questions are open-ended and seek to elicit reactions about specific elements of your business's customer care efforts.

- *Stay in "moderator" mode.* This is not a forum for selling or explaining why you've chosen to do things in a particular way. This is a time for listening. You should be engaged but not directive. Make it clear to everyone in attendance that you're there primarily to listen.

- *Get clarification when necessary.* If a participant is ambiguous or needs to be more specific, don't hesitate to ask clarifying questions. When you do, however, make certain your questions are not posed in a way that might be construed as challenging, judgmental, or confrontational. It is important for you to stay as neutral as possible. If you cannot do so, or if you feel your presence as the business's owner might stifle candid discussion, then have someone else moderate the discussion while you just listen.

- *Record the proceedings unobtrusively.* Let your participants know the conversation is going to be recorded, then videotape the discussion as inconspicuously as possible. The tape will be an invaluable tool for your team to use in evaluating the results.

- *Allow each participant to find his or her own level of participation.* Some of your participants will be more vocal than others. Make sure everyone has the opportunity to speak but don't insist on an arbitrary level of participation. The quality of participation is more important than the quantity. Keep your participants relaxed and as comfortable with the conversation as possible.

- *Be sure to thank your participants.* Don't forget this simple courtesy. Regardless of whether you've compensated participants or not, each one should receive a personal thank-you at the end of the proceeding

SOME CLOSING THOUGHTS ABOUT KILLER CUSTOMER CARE

HELP YOURSELF BY HELPING YOUR CUSTOMERS

Killer customer care is a great deal like the late Supreme Court Justice Potter Stewart's definition of obscenity. It's difficult to describe exactly, but you know it when you see it.

Starbucks has it. Most of its competitors don't. Nordstrom's has it. So does Virgin. But even though killer customer care is as recognizable as an old friend when you see it, it's still damned difficult to deconstruct into a formula.

We've looked at a number of strategies and tactics that can help you produce killer customer care in your business. What this book does not—and cannot—provide for you is the vision of what your particular end result will look like when you achieve it in your business.

This task is all the more challenging because killer customer care may never yet have been achieved in your industry or in your marketplace. You could become the Sir Edmund Hillary of your industry, the first to ascend to the peak of the Mount Everest of customer care. And although there's more glory in being the first, the trailblazer's path is always more difficult than the path of those that follow.

Don't Get Discouraged

Don't allow yourself to become discouraged or to despair because you can't find any role models. All of the pioneers of killer customer care were once in the same position.

When L. L. Bean decided to offer a lifetime guarantee on his "Bean Boot," he didn't have a great deal of precedent to guide him. He just figured his customers would appreciate being able to buy his products with absolute confidence. You probably couldn't have found a single accountant back then who thought that was a good idea. (In fact, you probably still can't today.) But it seems to have worked out well for Mr. Bean's business.

The only way to use this book effectively is to apply its principles to your own unique vision. Only then can the ideas presented here provide useful strategies and tactics for turning your vision into reality. And remember, a book that says it knows *exactly* what killer customer care should look like in your business might be inclined to fib about other things, too.

The publisher of this book, Entrepreneur Press, has its own procedures to achieve killer customer care, one of which involves using readers to evaluate a manuscript while it's in progress. As this book went through that process, one of the readers provided favorable feedback but noted parenthetically that the value of customer care is somewhat self-evident.

Ah, don't we all wish *that* were true?

Forget, for a moment about your role as a manager or entrepreneur. Think, instead, about your role as a consumer and customer. Do you regularly find yourself on the receiving end of killer customer care? Or do you find business after business interacting with customers in ways that could be described as disinterested, arrogant, incompetent, hostile, or rigid?

Everyone is eager to pay lip service to killer customer care, but few are willing to put forth the effort and focus necessary to make it happen. It's simple, but it's certainly not easy.

The good news, though, is that killer customer care represents a genuine opportunity for those businesses that are willing to do what it takes to achieve it and are steadfast enough to follow the guidelines in this book to implement their own visions of superior customer care.

Reread this book a couple of times. Of course, just reading it, or even rereading it, is not enough. Follow the steps outlined in its pages—one at a time, developing your own unique vision of customer care as you do.

Evangelize like crazy and get your employees on board. Then give your customers the ride of their lives. Make them say, "Wow!" Give them more reasons than they can count to keep coming back. Make your business so appealing, so comfortable that your customers can't resist telling their friends, family, and colleagues about it. Of course, try watching at the same time your business and your profits grow.

The strategies and tactics in this book can make all of that happen for you, but only if you give them a chance. Killer customer care is not a spectator sport. On the other hand, anyone can play.

That's the funny thing about it. Anyone who is determined to achieve killer customer care can make it happen.

Like you, for example.

SOME CLOSING THOUGHTS ABOUT KILLER CUSTOMER CARE / 237

INDEX